INNOVATION BY DESIGN

How Any Organization Can Leverage
Design Thinking to Produce Change,
Drive New Ideas, and
Deliver Meaningful Solutions

THOMAS LOCKWOOD AND EDGAR PAPKE

CAREER
PRESS
Wayne, NJ

INNOVATION BY DESIGN
Edited by Jodie Brandon
Typeset by PerfecType
Printed in the U.S.A.

To order this title, please call toll-free 1-800-CAREER-1 (NJ and Canada: 201-848-0310) to order using VISA or MasterCard, or for further information on books from Career Press.

The Career Press, Inc.
12 Parish Drive
Wayne, NJ 07470
www.careerpress.com

Library of Congress Cataloging-in-Publication Data

CIP Data Available Upon Request.

Our work is dedicated to the Creative Class. By the way, that's everyone.

CONTENTS

The Context

10 Attributes

The Context

1

Better Innovation

"Imagination is more important than knowledge. For knowledge is limited to all we now know and understand, while imagination embraces the entire world, and all there ever will be to know and understand."
—Albert Einstein

The collective imagination is humankind's greatest genius. Throughout our human history, as we developed and created the world around us, the sharing and building of one idea on another has been, and always will be, our best recipe for innovation. The world we continuously create for ourselves is the manifestation of our collective imagination, the natural desire to come together in community; to collaborate, explore, and learn; and to create what we want and desire to have. It gives us the ability to respond to our basic needs, as well as solve even the most complex of problems. It fuels the innovation that is the foundation of our competitive global business society. It is our collective imagination that provides us with the source of the innovation through which we create a better world and through which we find ways to guide and change the human experience. Humankind's desire and drive for innovation is breathtaking. Innovation is who we are. It is what we do best.

As our societies evolved, we creatively designed social structures that met the needs of and further relied on our shared ability to innovate. As we did, we were reminded that along with our innate desire to innovate, we have an inborn desire to compete. When these forces come together, innovation is accelerated. The social structures that we relied on for survival and connectivity evolved into enterprises of commercial means that have become the fixtures of our global society. These new enterprises and organizations became the vehicles that took us on the journeys of the scientific, industrial, and more recently information revolutions. All along the way, we continuously increased our level of innovation and ramped up the pace of change in our world.[1]

Today we find ourselves at a place in history in which our capability for innovating and creating change has provided us with incredible levels of technology and know-how. Every day we find ourselves exposed to new ideas. Moment by moment we are introduced to an array of new products and services, some of which are delivered to us by purpose-driven, design thinking organizations and enterprises whose main concern is to figure out how to create more meaningful innovation and customer experiences. We are now operating in a new global era in which a new digital economy is emerging—a new economy driven by pioneering technology that allows for virtually everyone and everything in our world to be connected, with new pathways for information and knowledge abounding: the Internet of Things, the interconnection via the Internet of computing and smart devices—electronics, software, sensors, actuators, and network connectivity—that enable objects to collect and exchange data. All this adds to a world that presents us with the means to faster and faster, innovate more and more—all evidence of how we leverage our collective imagination to creatively solve problems and meet the needs of humankind. Innovation is what we do best.

STRUGGLING WITH INNOVATION

With all the knowledge and technology available to us, and the means of immediate communication and instant access to information at our fingertips, why does our focus constantly return to how we can become even more innovative, to solve bigger and more complex problems? Why does so much of our attention remain centered on finding ways to organize and work together better to further leverage our ability to innovate? Why is meaningful innovation the most important issue that organizations continue to grapple and struggle with?

Throughout the history of business, we have found ourselves trying to figure out how to maximize our human potential. Even today, and more than ever, companies and institutions of all types and sizes are concentrating on creating more innovative cultures. This is not a new breakthrough in thinking. Being successful has always relied on the ability to work together and be creative. More than science or the collection and use of data, the quest to understand how to create higher levels of innovation and empower our creative intelligence seems to be a more elusive aspect of how we innovate. The better we become at innovation and creative collaboration, the more we want to figure out to get better at it—alas, human nature.

> Purpose-driven, design thinking organizations and enterprises create more meaningful innovation and customer experiences.

In pursuit of innovation, we have created complex organizations, with many moving parts, all adding to the complexity of our solutions, of our lives—until we come to the place of recognizing what the great designer Dieter Rams pointed out many years ago: "less, but better."

As complex as the world is today, we look for finding solutions to the resulting challenges and emotional stress that all the moving parts and advanced technology creates. The more complicated means of communication and interaction move us to a place from which we seek greater simplification. We have arrived at a place in our history that causes us to pause and reflect on the complexity of the organizational systems that humankind has created, looking for ways to overcome the needless barriers to communication and working together they represent. Why? So we can find better, faster, and, yes, simpler ways to work together to solve problems more efficiently and effectively. We want to innovate how our organizations can work more simply and allow for shared capacity to solve problems and innovate more freely.

To give you a sense of the magnitude of how important innovation is perceived to be to the success of today's organizations, one just has to look at the title of KPMG's 2016 Global CEO survey, aptly titled "Now or Never." The executive summary delivers a clear message, sharing that "[t]wo-thirds of chief executive officers (CEOs) believe that the next three years will be more critical than the last fifty years. The forces creating this inflection point are the rapidly evolving technology and the speed of transformation it unleashes. In four years' time 4 out of 10 CEOs expect to be running significantly transformed companies."[2]

A review of the results of a number of global surveys of CEOs, C-level executives, and leaders from 2015 to 2017, including the major studies conducted by KPMG, Fortune, IBM, and PwC, provide further insight.[3] With the exception of the Fortune survey (500 companies), most of the surveys we reviewed included more than 1,200 participants. Among the key findings:

- Fostering innovation is one of their top strategic priorities, placing among the top six in every survey.
- Most CEOs are grappling with how to engage their cultures in the change necessary to be more innovative.
- A significant majority (seven out of 10 CEOs) say it's important to specifically include innovation in their business strategies.
- The majority of survey respondents identify the need for transformational change in their organizations.
- Eight out of 10 are concerned that their existing products and services may not be relevant in three to five years' time.
- The majority of respondents say their organizations are struggling with the speed of technological innovation.

- Gartner reports that 89 percent of companies believe customer experience will be their primary basis for competition in 2016, versus 36 percent four years ago.
- Accenture reports that 81 percent of executives surveyed place the personalized customer experience in their top three priorities for their organization, with 39 percent reporting it as their top priority.

What is equally as telling is that, while innovation is consistently among the top six strategic priorities, less than a third believe their organizations' cultures encourage risk-taking or safe-to-fail environments. This is important to recognize. Among the more powerful aspects of motivation and human behavior are the needs for predictability and safety. From childhood through to adulthood, we are literally taught, trained, and reinforced to find the safest paths. As a result, satisfying these needs is paramount to how people perceive the ability to express themselves and take risks. We discover that it's not a good idea to tempt failure.

However, the process of innovation includes failure. Whether an organization's temperament and messaging allow for exploration, experimentation, and the potential subsequent failure says a lot about how innovative an environment it provides for its members. It also doesn't always fall within the context of processes and systems that are designed to limit risk. Or, ways of solving problems and making decisions that advocate adherence rather than possibility thinking. This is about culture. This is about the pursuit of understanding human behavior and the role that awareness plays.

These challenges are clearly defined in the KPMG report of findings:

- Thirty-six percent of CEOs say their organization's approach to innovation is either ad hoc, reactive or occurs on a silo basis.
- Only one out of four says that innovation is embedded in everything they do.
- Only 29 percent feel that their organization is highly capable of creating a safe-to-fail environment.[4]

This data becomes even more powerful when one considers that only one out of five CEOs note that innovation is at the top of their organizational agendas. This last piece of insight tells us that when identifying an organization's key strategic priorities, a top-six finish is likely still not good enough. Why? The most likely explanation is that, for CEOs and leaders, and the people in the companies and institutions they lead, the risk of being innovative is often what keeps their cultures from being more innovative. They are afraid of the risk of failure that comes from thinking outside the box, letting go of the familiar, seeking the possible over the predictable, all while falling into the trappings of that which they perceive will keep themselves safe. This is a stark reminder that, as a leader, if you're not willing to fail, others will not take a risk to succeed.

The data also raises the question of how the most successful organizations in the world go about innovating at the level they do, disrupting industries and market segments, quickly turning what were just yesterday stable technologies and ways of life into quickly outdated or obsolete ones. How do they go about creating new forms of industry and markets where none existed? How do they create more meaningful customer experiences and work across internal silos? What is the code to cracking their culture, and what do they do that is so different from the also-rans that they outperform? What are they doing that others aren't? How did they identify the gap between the average and the means to becoming exceptional innovators?

THE PATH OF CURIOSITY AND LEARNING

The questions at the end of the previous section were at the center of the conversation when, on a sunny, warm afternoon in Boulder, Colorado, in April 2016, we talked over a cup of coffee. Little did we know that moment would lead to conducting more than 70 interviews, extensive research and synthesis, co-creating frameworks, and, more than a year later, writing this book. As background, we have a personal relationship going back some two decades, have always been friends, and have always liked one another's work. We like to engage in philosophical conversations about life, which most of the time ends up being about creativity, business, and innovation. We've always spent a great deal of time talking about helping organizations and their leaders find ways to align to their purpose, solve the big problems of business, function better, and innovate at higher levels.

Between the two of us, we have the shared experience of more than five decades in the world of business consulting and coaching. Tom's work has been mostly focused on design, design thinking, and innovation, helping companies build great design, UX, and innovation organizations. In fact, he is one of only a handful of people on the planet with a PhD in design management. Edgar's focus is on understanding human motivation, organizational alignment, and leadership, coaching leaders and consulting with organizations on how to find and align to their purpose, and build and lead high-performing cultures. The themes that emerged from our conversations about business most often centered on the topics of design, innovation, culture, and the art of business. And, what the future may look like.

As coincidence would have it, on that sunny spring day, Edgar had recently returned from a trip to New Zealand and was excited about the work he had been doing with New Zealand Trade and Enterprise (NZTE), an experience he described as ridiculously fun and fulfilling. NZTE is the New Zealand government's international business development agency. Its purpose is to help New Zealand businesses grow bigger, better, and faster in international markets. Though this may sound like an obvious undertaking for any national government, the importance of its work cannot be overstated. To put it into perspective, one has to realize the magnitude of the scope of the effort involved and how important its outcomes are to the future of a nation that is remote to the rest of the world, has limited natural resources, and is dependent on the capability of its people and businesses to innovate. The only substantial economic growth, and that which the nation of New Zealand is dependent on for its future, is in the global marketplace. No doubt, innovation is at the heart of its success.

NZTE's work is focused on increasing New Zealand companies' international success by helping them boost their global reach and build their creative capability. In the end, the more successful international businesses grow, the more the nation's economy grows and benefits all

New Zealanders, providing jobs and raising the standard of living. One of the ongoing efforts and goals of NZTE is to "spark innovation."

Using Edgar's True Alignment framework to align the whole of NZTE to its purpose and branding, the organization brought together more than 130 of its key leaders. The main focus was to engage in the intentional alignment of the organization's global culture—and to explore how, as leaders, they would align their behavior and influence to that alignment. Peter Chrisp, CEO of NZTE, and his team named the leadership summit "The Hillary Step," likening the challenge the group had undertaken to the final ascent of Mount Everest by Sir Hillary and the first climbers to summit Mount Everest. They got it right. The Hillary Step unfolded as an engaging story line and served as a powerful metaphor.

What struck Edgar most was the capability of the attendees to engage in elements of design thinking to arrive at their outcome. Their ability to collaborate, take risk, quickly create and iterate, engage in creative activities, and openly express their thoughts and ideas was a reflection of not only their commitment to a shared purpose; it was also a manifestation of the influence of their use of design thinking, their chosen methodology used to arrive at identifying the key challenges to creating their ideal culture, and creating the solutions and exploring what was necessary to overcome their own challenges, as well as those of their customers. It was evident that their pursuit of fearless exploration and free-wheeling imagination were the direct result of their experiences in the use of design thinking and high-level capability to be innovative.

At the same time, Thomas was paying attention to emerging trends in the design business world. He was observing the increasing number of companies and consulting firms that were acquiring many of the best design firms. At the outset, he saw and predicted that the idea of design, and the methodology of design thinking, would eventually take hold in more and more companies, and was likely going to hold center stage and emerge as a primary means to drive innovation and change in organizations. Because of the need to deliver meaningful customer experiences at every touch point, organizations now have to include many skill sets, from business to technology, to engineering, to design, UX, systems, and services. What has stood out over the past decade is the way in which organizations were increasingly relying on design thinking to get higher levels of involvement and engage a broader set of stakeholders and competencies. More and more, they were using it as the means to attain higher levels of collaboration to solve problems and generate new ideas, resulting in an increased capability to create innovative solutions.

Design had already been well established as a means to achieve higher performance. A 2015 study by the Design Management Institute demonstrates that a set of larger design-driven companies (including Apple, Starbucks, Disney, and Nike) outperform the S&P 500 by 211 percent. Many similar studies previously conducted by Northeastern University in Boston, Red Dot in Germany, the British Design Council, the Industrial Design Society of America, and Thomas Lockwood have shown similar results.[5] The collaborative and creative means design leaders and design thinkers added to their organizations are not only critical to bringing new ideas, products, and services to market, resulting in higher levels of financial performance. They are also responsible for the disruptions that result in the creation of new markets. With all this attention to design, and design thinking growing in popularity for most of the past decade, two significant trends had emerged.

The first trend is that design is more and more becoming a readily adopted strategy by companies for responding to the need for innovation, differentiation, and customer experience. Coinciding with this trend, not only were companies beginning to see design as a core strategy essential to their success, they appeared to be adopting it as a core competency. Because a rising tide lifts all the ships, companies need good design in order to compete. There is a powerful extra benefit to the companies investing in design organizations: With more sophisticated design leadership and operations comes more sophisticated design thinking capabilities. We think this is both serendipitous and strategic, because the second trend that emerged was the race to build the competency of design thinking. In addition to building their design competency internally, some were willing to invest in buying it, thereby increasing both the immediate level of experience and dramatically speeding up the application of design thinking in their organizations.

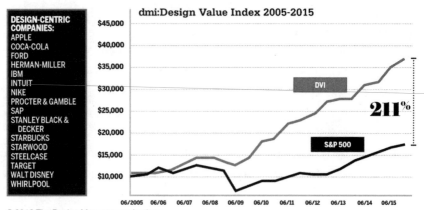

DESIGN-CENTRIC COMPANIES:
APPLE
COCA-COLA
FORD
HERMAN-MILLER
IBM
INTUIT
NIKE
PROCTER & GAMBLE
SAP
STANLEY BLACK & DECKER
STARBUCKS
STARWOOD
STEELCASE
TARGET
WALT DISNEY
WHIRLPOOL

dmi:Design Value Index 2005-2015

DVI

211%

S&P 500

06/2005 06/06 06/07 06/08 06/09 06/10 06/11 06/12 06/13 06/14 06/15

© 2016 The Design Management Institute

Between 2004 and 2016, more than 70 notable design and creative consulting firms had been acquired. Some of the early investments were Flextronics International taking a majority equity position in Frog Design and Steelcase taking a major equity position in IDEO, with Facebook, Square, and Google also picking up creative firms. What the next decade shows is a steady, yet somewhat small increase in the number of acquisitions. Then beginning in 2013, not only did the pace significantly increase, an important trend emerged: The major consulting firms of Accenture, Deloitte, KPMG, PwC, McKinsey, and Boston Consulting Group made acquisitions of top-notch design and creative agencies.

This was followed by another meaningful occurrence that has gained a lot of people's attention: More than 50 percent of all the acquisitions took place from 2015 to 2016.[6] And the players now included big companies, including IBM, Capital One, Airbnb, Salesforce, and Cooper. This is coupled by a hiring frenzy; as of the writing of this book, Accenture, Deloitte, GE, and IBM are all rumored to be hiring 1,000 designers each.

What Tom was observing and rightfully paying attention to was a very telling trend. Some would call it the starting gun to a race—the race to use design thinking as competitive advantage in accelerating innovation and investing in a new type of innovation readiness. Much like Edgar's compelling experience with NZTE, it appeared

COMPANY | DESIGN/CREATIVE AGENCY ACQUISITIONS

Company	Design/Creative Agency Acquisitions
Accenture	Fjord, Altitude, Karmarama, Reactive, Chaotic Moon, PacificLink
BBVA	Spring
Capgemini	Farenheit 212
Capital One	Adaptive Path, Monsoon
Deloitte	Doblin, Uselab, Banyan Ranch, Mobiento, Heat
EY	Intuitive
McKinsey	Lunar, Everyday, Carbon 12
PwC	Optimal Experience
Salesforce	AKTA Design, Gravity Tank

that design thinking was being identified as a missing link through which organizations were increasing their capability to innovate and create meaningful customer experiences. Let's just say that the early adopters were the first out of their starting blocks, and the race was on. Were we observing a business megatrend in the making?

This trend raised other curiosities for us. What effect was the emphasis on design reaching new heights and the increasing use of design thinking, as the means to increasing the capability of organizations to innovate, having on the organizations using it? How are they going about building their design thinking competencies? What effect does the use of and adopting and embedding design thinking in an organization have? Not just on its performance, but also on its culture? And how was it changing the thinking and behavior of leadership? How was it impacting employees?

In reflecting on the NZTE experience, what we experienced in working with innovative companies, and our shared work of the past several decades, we arrived at the conclusion that what we were observing was the convergence of three key elements: innovation, culture, and design thinking.

We then asked ourselves: If we explored and researched our ideas further, would it:

- Result in bringing something of value to the world that will make it a better place?
- Make a contribution to society?
- Respond to the need of business and social leaders whose priority is to be innovative?
- Help organizations find ways to solve the big problems of business?
- Create a better understanding of how organizations can better function and innovate at higher levels?
- Help leaders discover how to better engage others in being innovative?
- Capture and leverage employee creativity?

We believed the answer to these questions was *yes*. We then decided to find out what highly innovative companies that were significantly utilizing design thinking were up to, and if what they were doing would provide valuable insight into how any organization can use design thinking to produce change, drive new ideas, deliver meaningful solutions, and influence their culture to be more innovative.

2

Design Thinking Organizations

"In the beginner's mind there are many possibilities, but in an expert's mind there are few."
—Shunryu Suzuki

When we concluded that our shared interest had a clear purpose and could possibly bring something of value to the world, we set out to explore our ideas. That being said, as with any research project, we knew what we thought were good ideas might very well turn out not to be. We also recognized, and anticipated, the possibility of finding unexpected information. *All the better,* we thought.

We started our research by identifying a study group of organizations that have some of the most extensive and advanced-use design thinking on the planet. The sample was peer selected. That is, after we identified the first few world-class companies, they led us to others, and so on, based on the design thinking initiatives they admired the most. Once we had the organizations identified and engaged, we set out to understand to what level they were using design thinking, how they were implementing it, and what impact the adoption of design thinking was having on their cultures. The latter of these also offered us the opportunity to explore the ways in which an organization's culture influenced how they were using design thinking. Tom's observations on the increasing rate of how companies were adopting the use of design thinking led us to think we'd find a good correlation between the use of design thinking and their level of innovation.

We also decided that the organizations that we would include in our study had to have measurable success beyond just a financial or economic one. We took into consideration their performance as reflected by the triple bottom line: the delivery of social, environmental, and financial benefit. When it comes to innovation, the magic three of better, fast, and cheaper are often top of mind. We were also interested in the longer-term outcomes of the three Ps (people, planet, and profit).

As history has proven, by itself, financial gain or economic accomplishment is not always a good indicator of the innovativeness of an organization—especially not in today's world, in which the nature of human purpose and meaning are being explored at deeper and deeper levels of thinking. Nor is financial success always a good indicator of longer-term success. Of the companies considered the business world's great performers just a few years ago, today many are no longer relevant or even in existence (think Circuit City, Pitney Bowes, Blockbuster). The lessons learned are obvious. You must be innovative, and be able to have the ability to move and shift quickly, reinvent, and pay closer attention to the customer and their expectations. Keeping a singular focus on financial outcome and seeking monetary predictability, though at times warranted, can be costly and can have a negative effect on the innovative needs of an organization. And, keeping with approaches to business that sustained and even grew organizations a couple or so decades ago is likely not going to get you there today. The art of business is an ever-evolving one.

Using a more holistic approach to defining success also meant being open to evaluating the accomplishments of any organization as measured against their own and unique definition of success. In a world in which rapidly changing and shifting ideals of how business success is being measured are in play, we thought it important to consider all possibilities. Doing so also allowed for the inclusion of organizations we found to be highly innovative, very successful, and not typically included in the lists based solely on financial performance.

WHAT IS DESIGN THINKING?

As Thomas points out in his book *Design Thinking,* there are several key tenets that appear to be common in design thinking, and that we find consistently present in our design thinking organizations. The first is a quest to identify the right problem to solve, coupled with a deep understanding of the user. This is achieved through observation, fieldwork and research, an empathetic approach to discovering stated plus unarticulated user needs, and open inquiry. Rather than adding the dilemmas of missing the mark in understanding consumers' wants and needs, taking the approach of design thinking makes understanding the problem and the desired outcome all that much more focused and faster. As Tom points out, "The key is to start from a seeking to understand point of view."[1]

The second tenet of design thinking is empathy coupled with collaboration, both with the users and through the forming of multidisciplinary teams. In collaboration, constraints can be removed and great ideas can emerge. This helps to move an organization past silos and toward radical collaboration, rather than incremental improvement, thereby moving faster toward the creation and delivery of the right solution, a valued solution.

The third is to accelerate learning through hands-on experimenting, visualization, and creating quick rough prototypes, which are made as simple as possible in order to get usable feedback. Because design thinking is effective in radical problem-solving as well as incremental improvement, the more experimentation the better. The quick and simple prototypes also help grasp a potential implementation well before resources are spent in development. Often the goal is to fail quickly and frequently so that learning can occur. Prototypes can be sketches, rough physical mock-ups, stories, role-playing, concept storyboards—anything to help make the intangible more tangible. In a world in which shorter and abbreviated written messaging, visual cues, and emotional storytelling are overtaking written forms of communication, visualization has become a primary tool in the engagement of innovative thinking.

Lastly, Tom is a big advocate of integrating business model innovation during the process of design thinking, rather than adding later or using it to limit creative ideations. It's a delicate balance, but also one of the attributes of effective design thinking organizations. That is, they are able to integrate thinking by combining the creative ideas with business aspects, including the three Ps, in order to learn from a more complex and diverse point of view. This is also helpful in anticipating what new business activities and the resources that may be required in implementation of a new product, service, or experience initiative.

There are many definitions of design thinking floating around, but to be honest they are all pretty much the same. That's because design thinking itself is an open, shared, and co-developed concept. So let's not get wrapped up in semantics. According to Wikipedia:

> Design thinking refers to creative strategies designers utilize during the process of designing. Design thinking is also an approach that can be used to consider issues, with a means to help resolve these issues, more broadly than within professional design practice and has been applied in business as well as social issues. Design thinking in business uses the designer's sensibility and methods to match people's needs with what is technologically feasible and what a viable business strategy can convert into customer value and market opportunity.[2]

THE STUDY GROUP

Rather than thinking of highly innovative organizations as the most popular or biggest organizations that are ranked by revenue, capital value, or shareholder return, we focused on identifying a set of design thinking organizations that are peer-recognized as being among the most advanced in scaling and applying design thinking. Some of the companies we included also appear on the most innovative lists as compiled by *Forbes*,[3] *Fast Company*,[4] *Inc.*,[5] and *Fortune*.[6] We also included a few organizations that we felt deserved to be a part of our study, including the New Zealand Trade and Enterprise (see Chapter 1), Eleven Madison Park (see Chapter 15), and the Hunger Project (see Chapter 10). It's important to note that we did not qualify the organizations by industry or size, or categorically by purely their financial performance. That said, the organizations in our study can be regarded as highly innovative. Each, in its own way, by delivering to their purpose and in delivering in innovative ways, is an extraordinary achiever.

Lastly, and as you can see from the selections for our study, design thinking can be applied to any organization, of any size, in any industry to drive higher levels of innovations and performance.

We researched published examples of how each uses design thinking and conducted more than 70 interviews with members of the

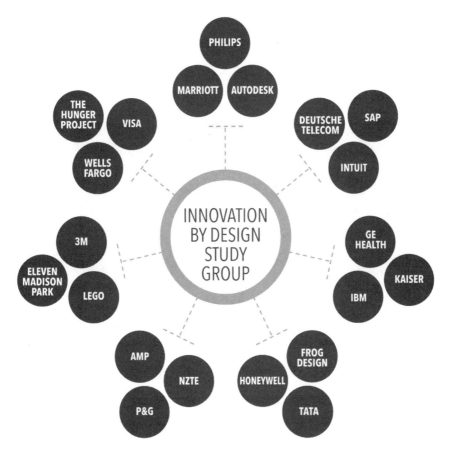

organizations such as CEOs, executives, internal human resources and organizational development practitioners, design thinking experts, design leaders, and CDOs (chief design officers). At our broader level of inquiry, among a host of questions and interests, our research and interviews analyzed how these organizations apply design thinking to:

- The design and creation of products, services, and experiences.
- The design of organizational processes, systems, and structures.
- The influence of design thinking on the organization's culture.
- The creation and leadership of longer-term strategy to drive innovations and performance.
- The functioning of teams, decision-making, and conflict resolution.
- The design of collaborative environments.
- The use of design thinking experts and consultants.
- The training and development of personnel.

As you might expect, our research and interviews led to unexpected areas and subjects of great interest and learning. We also got confirmation that, among the design thinking organizations we included in our study, they share a significant set of common traits and characteristics. And, though the organizations share a set of shared attributes, we also discovered and learned about the unique ways that design thinking is being used in, and integrated into, these organizations. These we found to be the result of influences in their cultures and leadership, as well as the outcomes they were seeking.

Exploring how the organizations use design thinking in different ways provides insight into the significance of being able to implement and integrate design thinking in a manner that aligns to the organization's culture—a mighty reminder that one size does not fit all is an incredibly powerful truth. This insight is one of the constant threads in realizing design thinking's influence on the creation and development, and leadership, of innovative cultures.

In our synthesis, we identified a set of 10 attributes that give remarkable power to the human-centered aspects of design thinking in these organizations. These represent core qualities that are required and through which other traits of innovative organizations come to life. They are the qualities that separate the truly innovative from those that strive to be like them.

The context for the 10 attributes is an organization's culture, which provides the means through which each attribute becomes an ingredient in the recipe for the successful pursuit of innovation. What brings all this to life and makes it all happen is the collective imagination: the energy created by human motivation. The motivation and drive of people to come together and participate in the pursuit of knowledge and the open sharing of ideas result in the creative and critical thinking that feeds innovation.

Putting these attributes into a process-oriented model of stages would be too contrived and not true to the reality of how things really happen. The attributes that follow can become parts of the context of how organizations use and integrate design thinking, some more quickly than others. As a result, our goal is to provide you with a framework and, in the chapters that follow, an understanding of their influence and importance. We provide some examples and ideas as to how to apply them to any organization or team to bring the traits of design thinking to life.

THE 10 ATTRIBUTES

Design Thinking at Scale

We went into our study focusing on organizations that, in one form or another, are using design thinking as a source of innovative thinking, execution, and performance. We didn't expect the scale to which some of the companies and organizations were applying it. Among the innovators the scale varied, as did the manner in which they implemented and integrated it. In some of the companies, design thinking was strategically seen as a function, a means through which to engage its membership on a larger scale. In others, we observed how design thinking spread, adding a belief in innovation and dramatically increasing its value. In some, it was approached from the top down. In others, it started as means to which to solve a particular problem in one part of the organization, and people were naturally drawn to its qualities and wanted in on the game. In still others, it was a part of human resources and organizational development strategies that were delivered through training and facilitation. What was consistent is that, regardless of how it was happening, how it was introduced, implemented, and integrated, people are drawn to participating in design thinking.

The Pull Factor

We discovered that one of the essential attributes of innovative cultures is what we call the "pull factor." The best way to describe the pull factor is by defining it as the emotional momentum that results from the natural consequence of people wanting to engage and be part of innovation and the design thinking experience. And the pull factor appears relevant in all generations: Generation Z, Millennials, Generation X, even Boomers. It certainly differs from the more traditional ways in which organizations have viewed how they try to engage their members and drive innovation. This requires leaving behind the multitude of failed processes and systems that merely repositioned the methods of the past—the approaches that, unfortunately, invited people to venture down the path of the fallacy that the best way to solve a problem was to eliminate human emotion. What truly innovative organizations do is quite the opposite. They leverage one of the most important elements of human creativity and the foundation of the human art of business. They leverage emotion.

The Right Problems

A common trait of design thinking cultures is their aim to identify and solve the root causes of problems, in addition to the short-term success of low-hanging fruit. The organizations in our research are not driven to just creating new ideas. Rather, they have a need for better ideas and finding the right innovation. Design thinking cultures are not about just brainstorming or ideation, they are about developing a competency to *identify and then focus on what is important, and to solve that.* At its best, finding the right problem means focusing on the customer, the user. The end game of any business, of any organization, is to deliver something of value to the key recipient who has a need or want of something—a problem that needs to be solved. The organizations in our study group are compelled to go to the core and be challenged. They understand that there's nothing like a good challenge to motivate innovation. It turns the dare of risk taking into fun. It also turns into the energized pursuit and fulfillment of a purpose.

Cultural Awareness

Like a lot of processes and systems that are introduced or strategically implemented into an organization, design thinking can either take flight or fail to be integrated, lose traction, and fade away over time. Or, it can be seen as just another process and strategy in a long list of temporary fixes or another flavor of the day that management has decided will fix everything. There are a host of reasons this happens, including the lack of support from an organization's members and leaders. These are indicators of a far more powerful aspect of implementation: culture. Design thinking, like other ideas and strategic solutions, can fail. In the vast majority of cases, this is not the result of them being bad ideas. Rather, they fail to stick because they do not fit the culture of the organization or are not implemented in a manner that aligns with the organization. Why does it always have to be about culture? Because it is. We learned from our study that having organization empathy, and the ability to assess an organization's culture, is to better understand the essence of how it innovates. It is the strongest cure to overcoming the flavor-of-the-month syndrome.

Curious Confrontation

Because design thinking is a way of leading with creativity, it encourages embracing ambiguity, uncertainty, and curiosity. One of the greatest challenges any organization or team will face lies in how it effectively manages competing interests, differing views, disagreement, and conflict, all of which are natural contributors to innovation. One of the key advantages that the organizations in our study have in common is that design thinking offers a platform for the constructive management of diverse thinking and strategies. In spending resources to teach design thinking to their members and develop it as a core competency, they leverage the benefit they get from using it as a management tool for converting disagreement into fuel for creativity and innovation.

The reality is that every organization has its struggles in dealing with differing points of view, values, and beliefs. As a result, we don't generally listen to one another very well. Not only does design thinking provide a framework for people to express themselves, it also provides a platform for listening and empathy. Empathy, as displayed through genuine inquiry and expression, is paramount for users of design thinking and, as the result of lessened levels of fear, leads to the increased levels of emotional maturity and safety that directly impact how diverse views and ideas are constructively managed.

Co-Creation

One of the most powerful attributes of design thinking organizations is their ability to embrace co-creation. Despite the natural reliance on forms of functional structures and hierarchies, the organizations in our research are not bound by the limitations of their structure or the defined roles people find themselves in. Rather, they invite inclusion, and bring together diverse groups and parties to collaboratively produce mutually benefitting and jointly valued outcomes. Often, it includes customers, consumers, functional groups and teams, industry experts, and members throughout the organization. In most instances, their use of co-creation results in greater levels of information sharing, more timely and productive problem-solving, and better-informed employees, customers, and leadership, not to mention higher levels of engagement and loyalty among those involved, including customers.

Open Spaces

An aspect of strategically leveraging the attribute of open spaces is to think creatively about the use of space, technology, visual tools, and eventually the application of different forms of art. We expected to find the expressive handiwork in the making and use of environments and spaces that encouraged creative and open expression. This is a commonly expected attribute of highly innovative organizations and teams, and the organizations lived up to our expectations. In some cases, they surprised us with the ingenuity with which they created such environments. This includes what physical space looks and feels like, how virtual communities and teams use visual tools and technologies, and their effect and reinforcement of creative and collaborative behavior and open communication. The attribute of open spaces is also a means of the emotional expression that invites an open mind for creative expression and more open and meaningful dialogue. Open mental spaces enable strategic conversations.

Whole Communication

The companies in our study demonstrate an increased competency to communicate in highly creative ways. We were pleasantly surprised to find that they are great storytellers, and creators and users of visual information. They appear to understand that innovation does not happen by doing surveys and writing comprehensive reports or slide decks with facts and figures. Innovation happens by contextual inquiry, discovering unarticulated needs, synthesizing, creating with empathy, and communicating solutions in methods that embrace the emotions underlining the concepts. The visualization of information and storytelling of problems and solutions are paramount to success. They show an understanding that, when it comes to engaging stakeholders to embrace and contribute to the development of ideas and solving the right problems, emotion matters.

Aligned Leadership

We expected that the role of leadership would, along with culture, be an important element. And it is. However, what is more important is to understand the powerful influence that leaders convey through their involvement, role modeling, and strategic support. This is true whether someone is an outgoing leader and communicator, a quiet engineer, an A-type driver of performance and outcomes, a servant that thrives on being liked and loved, or a top-down planner and strategist. Regardless of style or role, they trust in the process of design thinking, engage in it, and advocate its use. Such leaders also expect the other leaders in the organization to follow suit. They are the primary catalysts for aligned leadership at the other levels of the organization, and have a significant influence on how teams function and deliver more innovatively.

Purpose

The organizations in our study demonstrate a sense of purpose in bringing something of value to the world. They show the ability to successfully integrate two key aspects of innovative success: the external focus on the customer and the internal focus on their cultures and how they do things. A commonsense approach to the tension that exists in the relationship between the two tells us that this is an obvious requirement to success. Much like individual human beings, organizations need to be aware of who they are in relationship to the world they live in. The simple truth is that, for any organization to be innovative, it must have a shared set of ideals as to its purpose for existence. Why? Because its members will be more engaged and possibility oriented in how they think and act.

MULTIPLYING CREATIVITY

As we identified the 10 attributes, we grappled with whether the pull factor belongs alongside the other nine attributes, or whether it deserves to be recognized as a separate element. Our decision to call it a factor reflects the multiplying effect that design thinking has on the breadth and level of participation. It not only results in greater numbers of people wanting to participate, it also multiplies and accelerates creativity, and the quantity and quality of ideas and potential solutions to problems. The more organizations make design thinking available, the more people are drawn to participating and the greater the level of innovation possible. This is very different from how organizations typically push or try to mandate innovation. When we explored why design thinking is an accelerator of participation in innovation and change, we found ourselves coming back to human motivation. This turned our attention to the idea of the collective imagination, and the sources of human motivation.

3

Collective Imagination and the Fifth Order of Design

"Life is short, but it can be wide."
—Thomas Lockwood

The human energy that brings the 10 attributes together to make things work is the collective imagination: the natural desire of human beings to come together in community—to collaborate, explore and learn, and create what we want and desire to have. It is the fuel that emanates from the core of who we are as people and provides the substance and underpinnings of our organizational cultures. The creative imagination provides the energy for creativity and innovation to freely flourish.

In Edgar's book *True Alignment,* he provides a model for better understanding the relationship and desired alignment of the customer experience and branding to the cultures of organizations and teams.[1] The psychology behind his model uses FIRO-Theory as the underpinning science. A powerful lens through which to see human behavior and its underlying motivation, FIRO-Theory was created by psychologist and author Will Schutz in the late 1950s.[2] Schutz

> FIRO-Theory suggests that all
> human behavior and interaction is motivated
> by three fundamental desires to feel:
> 1) Important and significant.
> 2) Competent and capable.
> 3) Liked and accepted.

correctly theorized that all human behavior and interaction is motivated by three fundamental desires to feel:

1. Important and significant.
2. Competent and capable.
3. Liked and accepted.[3]

These are the same elements that make up the motivational drivers of our human capability to innovate and act as the pillars of the collective imagination: participation, the pursuit of knowledge, and free expression.

THE COLLECTIVE IMAGINATION

Participation

In innovative organizations, we see the collective imagination at work through the behaviors of involvement, collaboration, and cooperation that result in the sharing of ideas, people paying attention to each other, and the subsequent sharing and leveraging of differing viewpoints, inferences, and opinions. The underlying influence that opens the door to the successful collaboration among the members of an organization or team is the human need for inclusion. If we dig a little deeper, we find that this natural need for participation and connectivity has a great deal of influence in how people feel valued and respected. This is what makes listening such a powerful aspect of

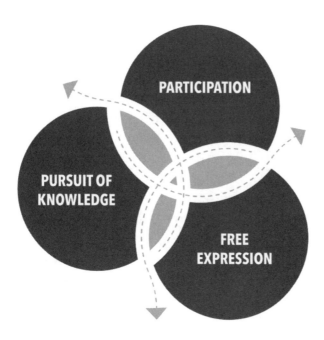

design thinking. When we feel like we will be paid attention to, and not ignored, we show up, get involved, and share our ideas.

Pursuit of Knowledge

Innovative cultures are always hungry for new ideas and thrive on finding new ways to understand our world and how human beings and nature function. Fueled by our innate desire to feel competent, and have a sense of control and wanting to know more and always do better, the pursuit of knowledge is the force of nature behind our ability to think critically, inquire, and ideate. This includes the analysis of data and the use of available criteria, and the seeking of new information to solve problems. In innovative cultures, analytics, data interpretation, and the creation of measurable feedback loops in the prototyping and iteration processes, are means through which a focus on expanding what we know and asking "What if?" questions exists. As human beings, we are never quite satisfied with what we have and know. The two are intertwined. To get more of what we want, we seek the knowledge necessary to create what we seek.

Free Expression

Our ability to freely express what we think, see, and feel, without the risk of being rejected or not being liked, offers the capability to engage in the unbridled creativity that results in the uninhibited generating of ideas, brainstorming, and the more imaginative and fearless expression of thoughts and feelings. The use of playful and artistic expression is evidence of this basic and yet powerful source of creativity. Fearless exploration is often at the heart of extraordinary innovations. It is important to recognize that free expression is the path through which we open ourselves to being vulnerable and intimate with one another, and express our feelings. In reciprocity, we are more apt to give empathy to those that allow us to communicate without inhibition or fear. Fearless expression is also one of the keys to imaginative communication. It provides us with the sense of childlike wonderment and deeper emotional connection to our work and our seeing business and innovation as art forms. It reminds us that business is art. And that art is the creative expression of human emotion.

Put the three pillars in place, and you have the ingredients that manifest in our collective imagination and that provide the underlying motivation for our constant and ongoing quest to innovate. As important as the three pillars are to the successful application of design thinking, they are also essential to highly innovative cultures. In light of this, it's important to note that you can't succeed by relying on one or two of the three. As fundamental as they are, they are also fully interdependent, and therefore essential to creating success. This is why design thinking plays such a significant part in how innovative cultures attain success.

Unlike many other processes that have come and gone, and that have the aim of bringing the power of the collective imagination to the forefront, none has been as successful as design thinking. This is evidenced by the level of problem-solving and innovation being achieved by the organizations using it.

THE FOUR ORDERS OF DESIGN

The evolution of design that has unfolded over the past century is likely best explained by Richard Buchanan's Four Orders of Design. Buchanan, a professor of design, management, and information systems, is cited as being one of the first people to talk about the development of the Four Orders of Design. As an organization matures in its use of design, it tends to move from communication and visual design, to products, to brands, to systems.[4] With the acceleration of changes in technology that advanced our capability to communicate and create a broader array of customer and user experience, the application of design also accelerated.

The first two orders of design emerged in the first half of the last century. The First Order focuses on graphic design and visual communication, including signs, symbols, and print. Today, this order is more and more focused on the design of more concise visual messaging, including web-based applications.

The Second Order focuses on the design of products, including their form and feel. One of the more popular examples is Apple's pursuit of rounded corners. This aspect of its product design is so important to the company that it filed for and, in 2012, was granted a design patent.

In the Third Order, Interaction, attention turned to the design of the client or customer experience and application in the design of services, user experiences and interfaces, and information.

Then, Buchanan summarized, in the Fourth Order, attention shifts to the design of systems in which people interact with one another, including businesses, organizations, education, and government. The latter of these is focused on the interaction of people with one another and the design of systems and environments. The Fourth order of design also addresses the idea of tackling wicked problems. The shift from designing products and services to designing systems includes the design of social systems, including organizations, that begin to take into consideration the role of culture.

THE FIFTH ORDER OF DESIGN

This brings us to recognition of the potential for the intentional design of cultures, and the design of learning itself, which presents a whole new array of problems to solve. Successfully designing culture requires a framework for identifying and exploring the various elements and characteristics of organizations and how people interact within. This carries with it a new set of design challenges that result from the need to understand human psychology and motivation. Whereas there's always been a natural integration of psychology in design, in the Fourth Order it began to take a more prominent role. Designing the systems of human interaction requires a significant level of insight into human motivation and desire. Depending on the size of the system, and the number of people and the patterns of behavior they engage in, this can become a complex undertaking.

Typically, to affect the cultures of our organizations, we rely on restructurings and the implementation of data-driven solutions as process improvement. This is merely scratching at the surface of culture change, let alone transformation. To successfully engage in the necessary level of change, or the design of culture, requires us to be able to deconstruct and reconstruct it, and to be able to understand how to create it anew.

When we talk about designing culture, we're setting the stage for designing the intentional interaction of people. And, we move from the intellectual exercise of organizational design to the emotional aspects of human behavior. This involves a keen understanding of *who* and *why,* resulting in the creative expression of *how.* The big upside to this pursuit is that we find ourselves with the opportunity to not only better integrate design and design thinking into culture, but to create more organizational learning and knowledge sharing, as well as create greater levels of emotional awareness.

How we have used design thinking has changed rapidly, and we now find ourselves responding to a new way of thinking and experiencing our world. More and more, we are questioning how and why we interact with one another in our organizations in the way we do. We question intention, purpose, and motivations. As we further develop our capacity to innovate, how and with whom we participate will expand and change. The shift to greater transparency requires us to more consciously design and develop the cultures and learning capacities of our organizations.

To this we add a global environment in which the relationships between companies and their customers are becoming more open and interlinked. Customers are becoming active members in the design of the products and services with the organizations they are buying them from, more and more, influencing how they are created, branded, sold, and delivered. With these shifts comes a new set of requirements for organizations, their leaders, and the people in them. More open systems and engaging means of participation are required.

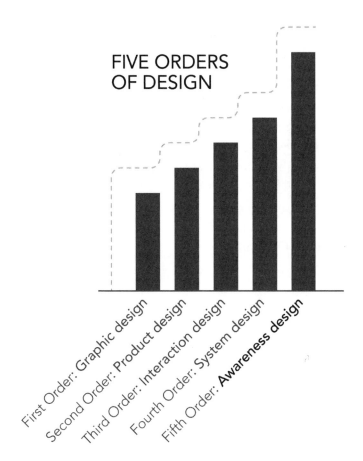

A new language for awareness will be needed to further the art of design and design thinking and take organizations to greater levels of creativity, innovation, and achievement. As we'll explore and demonstrate in the following chapters, design thinking not only provides a methodology that both naturally and intentionally leverages the collective imaginations and transforms cultures into being more innovative, it also provides a path to the intentional design of culture. Lastly, it provides design thinking organizations with the opportunity to step into the Fifth Order of Design: awareness. Design thinking organizations are learning organizations, and use design thinking to increase understanding and ultimately awareness—of the real problems, of customers, of obstacles, of options, of knowledge, and of one another. In effect, by using design thinking to empower creativity and collective imagination, organizations develop the means to step further toward what lies at the core of human-centered design: our basic human needs and motivation.

In the chapters to follow we'll delve deeper into the attributes of design thinking organizations and their cultures, and explore how the organizations in our study increased their innovative capabilities. We'll delve further into how the collective imagination builds learning and provides the motivational energy to bring them together to deliver a powerful recipe for change. And before we reach the end of this book, we'll take some time to share another one of the conclusions that we arrived at from our study: that design thinking organizations have before them the challenge and opportunity to achieve the Fifth Order of Design.

4

Designing Culture

"I came to see, in my time at IBM, that culture isn't just one aspect of the game, it is the game."
—Louis Gerstner

Transforming a culture requires changing individual and collective behavior. One of the greatest values to be gained from design thinking is the impact it can have on the culture of an organization and how it contributes to greater collaboration and innovation, regardless of its size.

GE is a good example. In 2016 the company's revenue topped $123 billion. GE has more than 330,000 employees operating in over 180 countries. It comes as no surprise that in a commentary published in April 2017, John G. Rice, the company's vice chairman, shared his observation that it's natural for a business of GE's size and scale to see silos manifest along the way. He pointed out that the sharing of ideas and collaboration necessary to be innovative, and the ability of employees to team to add new value, have always been a challenge for the company: "Without a radical shift in everyday working behavior—in employee's relationships with the company and one another—silos will remain, and the sort of cross-industry and horizontal collaboration that companies like GE need to foster for growth is not going to happen."[1]

For any organization to undergo the continuous change required to sustain and grow, and to be innovative, requires its leaders and employees to understand the tension between the paradigm of consistency offered by its culture and the ambiguity necessary for change. This means that they must be able to, at a root level, both trust in the necessity of their culture to evolve, while not relying on or creating unnecessary conditions of predictability.

It also requires being responsive to what is required to attract and leverage the ever-evolving world of talent. One of the keys to attracting creative talent is to create a culture that thrives on continuous learning and risk-taking. This requires creating shifts in the culture to interest the new generation in the workforce, a group that wants to engage in a set of work experiences that are radically different from those of the past—a set of experiences that call for the greater levels of participation, and more collaborative and fast-paced ways that design thinking affords. It is about a more creative and engaging way to work and innovate together.

In its effort to become more design thinking–focused, GE recently moved its headquarters to downtown Boston. Of the 800 positions at its new headquarters, 600 are designers, developers, and product managers—all evidence of the shift from being engineering-driven to design-driven, from product-centric to customer-centric, and from marketing-focused to user experience–focused. It's also a sign of the need for executives to collaborate more with designers, design thinkers, and design leaders.[2]

In a September 2016 interview with the Aspen Institute's Walter Isaacson, when asked about the rise of the creative class and the company's move to Boston, GE's CEO Jeff Immelt explained:

> I have to say it's real. I thought it was a little bit of B.S. initially, I wasn't sure. And when I looked out the window—when I was in Connecticut, it was beautiful, awesome, great

office—but when I looked out my window, I saw nothing, there was nothing going on. I could watch cars go on the highway, things like that. I've been [in] Boston now six weeks and you just walk out the door. You're in the middle of an ecosystem that quite honestly, for a big company, it makes you afraid. You're where the ideas are. You get more paranoid when you're doing that and that's a good thing.[3]

And how else is GE's new headquarters different? "The new headquarters will be leaner, faster and more open with a constant flow of industry partners, customers and innovators." The intent, execs say, "[i]s that it will be more like walking into a start-up in an urban setting than the remote suburban headquarters of the past," helping to transform its culture from a functionally driven one with silos, to a culture focused on collaborative design thinking and creativity.[4]

FROM FEAR TO TRANSFORMATION

What keeps us from realizing the tension between predictability and the ambiguity of change, the kind of real change that offers the opportunity for an organization to transform itself, and shift its culture?

Over time, it's an easy trap to fall into. Humans often favor the sense of control that not undertaking change provides. As a result, to protect ourselves from the risk and fear of the unknown, we also move further way from being aware of the emotional response to the challenges and need for change around us. This results in not paying attention to or sensing the world around us. With all the innovation that our quest for predictability and control affords us, we naturally create barriers to the change and innovation we seek.

Organizing to be competitive, and the resulting culture to deliver consistently through the years, establishes a powerful paradigm to how things "should" be done. It's important to recognize how this happens. Of the outcomes that evolved from the inception of scientific management and all the processes and systems that followed, organizations fell into the trap of using the innovations that were creatively devised to increase productivity and applied them to limit the very aspects of creativity that got them there. It was a double-edged sword that most did not see coming, and the dampening of creativity soon found its way into organizations of all types and sizes. For-profit, not-for-profit, social and government entities—they began suffering from a lack of empowered membership.

That doesn't mean that organizations became void of innovation. Leaders learned to rely on a rather isolated few people who found ways to solve problems and create innovative solutions. By relying on scientific-based innovators, generally in R&D or technical leadership roles, businesses continued to provide performance-based evidence that these approaches resulted in innovation. In fact, many organizations and their leaders still rely on approaches to organization and employee management that have been in silos and in use for close to two centuries. And even new/incoming leadership is expected to behave in the way that reinforces old status quo role models and their standard approaches.

Over time, and with the broadening use of design thinking, it's also become apparent that those old models don't work as well as we once thought. As a result, influenced by the changing world around them, leaders are now more than ever questioning how to make things different and exploring the true nature of what makes organizations perform and act more creatively—more innovatively. They are rediscovering that business is an art, and placing more emphasis on letting people act creatively and giving them the opportunity to engage in innovation and design thinking. This has opened the door to the need for better understanding culture.

For these reasons, in this chapter and the next, we thought it valuable to visit and look more closely at what culture is, and explore the unique forms it can take. We'll try to do this in a manner that doesn't rehash everything that's already out there and you may have already come across on the subject. In the last couple of decades, with the heightened awareness of the importance of culture and reminders that it eats strategy for lunch, you may have already satisfied your appetite. That being said, one of the more powerful traits of innovative people is their ability to think like beginners and avoid always thinking like and being the experts.

DESIGN THINKING AND CULTURE: UNIQUENESS MATTERS

The companies in our study group are all design thinking organizations. Therefore, throughout our research, we were brought back to the basic idea that one of the requirements to successfully implement design thinking to produce change and spark innovation is having a framework to understand culture. Understanding how design thinking can be applied and leveraged in any culture to manifest greater levels of innovation is a key to success. It turns out that design thinking is one of the best approaches to welcoming and creating culture change. To be successful, leaders and the people they lead will require a better understanding of the context they work in and a higher level of awareness of who they are in relationship to it.

What is needed is a definition of culture and a means through which to assess the various aspects of an organization's behavioral traits and leadership influence. What culture does more than anything else is inform and reinforce its members how to individually and collectively attain success. It's how to behave. The definition of what success is and how it happens is as unique to the organization as it is to an individual's role. Culture speaks to the various aspects of behavior associated with attaining success. It includes the behaviors that support achievement or get in the way of it, resulting in a set of expectations and an understanding as to what is acceptable and unacceptable behavior. The same applies to the behavior of teams.

> Culture informs people how to individually and collectively achieve success, communicating and reinforcing what is acceptable and unacceptable behavior.

Another way we refer to these aspects is to call culture by another name: politics. Let's keep in mind, the reality is that, despite the formal set of values that management may articulate and hang on walls, it's the informal rules of behavior that will yield greater influence on people and how they work together.

One of the more powerful aspects of design thinking is its influence on culture. All organizations and businesses, including those that are much smaller, will encounter similar problems. Yes, the bigger you get, the more complex and difficult communication and collaboration become. Yet if you look at it through the lens of what drives these potential outcomes, the path takes us back to human behavior. Cultures don't create people. People create cultures. In some cases, to create a shift toward being innovative requires a radical shift in employee behavior. It requires a change in the relationships employees have with the company and with one another.

We investigated a diverse set of design thinking organizations in a range of the different industries they successfully compete in. One thing became perfectly clear: When it comes to culture, one size does not fit all. In our shared experience working with organizations the world over, this is one of the primary reasons why leaders struggle with culture and leading change as much as they do.

Culture is unique to every organization. Yes, there are traits and characteristics that consistently show themselves and that we can identify and intentionally use. Some of these are strategic and are elements of the systemic design of an organization, intended to influence behavior and how things get done. Others are the natural result of the context and environment that influence behavior and occur in response to the underlying motivations we all share as human beings.

Changing and transforming a culture also set up the tension between the desired predictability of looking at it as a system that delivers and thrives on predictability and control, and one that is intended to manifest and thrive on disruption and freewheeling creativity. Though there are cultural elements that are common and applied with some reliability to most organizations, all too often what works for one organization's culture doesn't work for another. It's much like expecting a time management tool that works for one person to fit and deliver results to everyone else. We all know that for such a tool to be useful and create beneficial outcomes, and eventually change habits, it needs to fit a person's personality and therefore must be pliable.

The appeal of knowing and replicating other successful organizations presents another potential minefield of missteps, some of which are very difficult to recover from. Because something works at Disney doesn't mean it will work at Apple, and vice versa. And do they all, regardless of their size and geographic scope, face the issues similar to GE? It's valuable to know what traits are embedded in the cultures of organizations that have succeeded in innovating over the long haul, such as IBM, Lego, 3M, Disney, Philips, and Johnson & Johnson—organizations that remain true to the core of who they are, yet demonstrate the ability to innovate and reinvent, create changes to innovate their cultures, and keep their drive to be competitive.

THE 12 CULTURE KEYS

In Edgar's book *True Alignment*, he offers insight into the various forms that organizational cultures will take. He also identifies a set of 12 culture keys, human elements and strategic tools through which cultures are influenced. The 12 keys also provide the framework for defining culture and the key traits that are critical to guide the implementation of design thinking in a way that the culture will accept, implement, integrate, and embed. In other words, the more an organization and its leaders understand the culture keys and their influence, the better they are able to align its implementation and get the results they're looking for.[5]

There's more to this. From the design perspective, the culture keys provide insight and a set of considerations for the intentional design of culture. As we'll discuss and demonstrate later in this book, this makes the case for and demonstrates the use of design thinking in the intentional design and leadership of innovative cultures, and supports the Fifth Order of awareness design we presented in the last chapter. It's important to keep in mind the following keys can be applied in a host of different forms. Even more important is to recognize how each influences the use of design thinking in a particular unique culture.

Power and Influence

The origin of power and influence is one of the aspects of culture that is a major contributor to culture. It also provides insight into how leaders influence the activities and actions of the individuals, teams, and ultimately, the organization. To interpret the source of power and influence, we refer to the three sources of human motivation that we share in Chapter 2 and Chapter 3, and that have their roots in FIRO-Theory.

The first of these is the individual and team influence of expertise, knowledge, and competency. It is often reflected in level of authority granted to someone through title or rank (e.g., team lead, project owner, practice leader). In some instances, it can be further leveraged through the taking of control over situations that offer the opportunity to reinforce one's capability, know-how, competency, or proficiency.

The second distinctive source stems from one's ability to include and pay attention to others. Conveying importance and mutual respect is a powerful source of influence. Encouraging and inviting others to participate, and respectfully listening to them, is a means through which to gain influence.

Being seen as genuine and forthright, and acting out of a commitment to a set of higher values and beliefs, is the third distinctive source of power. Often, individuals who are transparent, seen as authentic, and act in alignment to a set of values and ideals that are in alignment to those of the culture will attain a high degree of personal power.

Planning and Goal-Setting

Planning and goal-setting processes typically have the same fundamental steps in common. What varies from culture to culture is how they are used. This is an important point, because the principles that are applied to the alignment of how planning and goal-setting are undertaken, apply to the alignment of the practices associated with design thinking. When we look at design thinking as change, we begin to realize the significance of its use in a planning process. While people are being asked to plan for change, if the manner in which they are asked to participate is familiar and engaging, it will provide an emotional anchor from which to plan and contribute to change.

Problem-Solving

All of the culture keys play a significant role in defining and articulating aspects of culture. And all are important to how people are influenced. That being said, when a group of people is unclear as to how to solve a problem and reach a decision, it can have significant consequences on just about everything else it endeavors to accomplish. It's paramount to understand how engagement in problem-solving affects how individuals relate to their own sources of motivation to feel heard and competent, and how open and honest they can afford to be. This is what makes design thinking such a valuable asset to any organization and its culture.

When it comes to problem-solving and decision-making, there is ample room for misinterpretation, confusion, and mistrust in the process. Often, the result is a lack of engagement in the identification and creation of possible solutions. Not having an inclusive process will also directly impact the level of commitment to the implementation of the solution.

Decision-Making

One of the major sources of predictability and strength in a culture comes from the sense of autonomy that people get from having the ability to make decisions. That being said, one of the major sources of conflict in companies and teams stems from the lack of clarity and alignment on how decisions are made. There are a host of considerations surrounding process, participation, and empowerment. For any culture, success requires clarity of who and how decisions are made.

Conflict Management

Of all the ways that we learn about the culture of a group or company, the one that often provides the most memorable lessons is how we experience conflict. This applies to both when we see others engaged in conflict or disagreement *or* we find ourselves, often unknowingly and unwillingly, engaged in it ourselves. The use of power and influence, rank, position, and role can all be observed in how conflict is managed, as well as listening, collaboration, and constructive problem-solving. How the creation of mutual benefit and winning and losing are perceived, and what values are most important to a culture, will often be tested in times of conflict.

Incentive and Reward

Recognition can come in different forms. It's important to know what the prevailing form is that is unique to a culture. In some cultures it's recognition in the form of participation and involvement; in others it may be flexibility in working hours, learning opportunities, or the motivation of being challenged. The popular approach is to align the incentive, reward, or celebration to the stated measurable goal. In the simplest terms, what is measured and rewarded gets done.

It is true that in some organizations the approach to incenting and rewarding is monetary. Then again, what we often learn the hard way is that doesn't necessarily mean it is the most effective or the most important to everyone. In general, if we are to try to argue the success of using money as the key reward, from either end of the spectrum of belief, we have a tough argument on our hands. That being said, we likely all agree that there is more to human motivation than money. It's just a matter of individual preference, motivation, and need, and what the culture is most aligned to.

What's important to remember is that unspoken expectations are the slippery slope to anger, resentment, and distrust. Therefore, it's important that people within any organization enjoy the clarity of knowing how they will be rewarded for their efforts, performance, and contribution to the whole.

Hiring

Extraordinary cultures learn to be really good at hiring the right people. The clearer the purpose, culture, and values of an organization, the more it is able to attract individuals that are good fits. There are two good reasons for this. The first is the emotional connection and affinity, on a conscious or subconscious level, that people feel. This includes the sense of alignment to the organization's purpose, brand intention, and desire to be involved and connected with it.

The second reason is that the members of an aligned culture are more apt to share their experience with others, creating an attraction among like-minded people seeking employment and new opportunity. This valuable asset is not to be overlooked. Some of the best recruiting isn't always achieved by human resources or by external recruiters. It is accomplished by the employees of companies who are their true believers and invest themselves in getting like-minded and talented people to the company.

Role Definition

Role definitions and how they align to culture hold several sources of emotional content. For one thing, role definitions are often tied to titles and a sense of personal achievement, or verification of one's place in a hierarchy. They can also respond to people's need for a sense of autonomy and an opportunity to further develop. When a person is given a team role, it confirms their membership and connectivity, a sense of belonging, and inclusion in a group or team. Lastly, a role definition can often provide evidence of who someone is or is a confirmation of who they aspire to be. It signifies proof of an individual's association with a cause or ideal that they wish to be connected to. In some instances, it confirms personal purpose.

Customer Interface

We're in a new digital economy. How a culture interfaces with the customer has changed dramatically over time. Along with advances in how we market and sell, the leveraging of technology and the media, and the innovations that have propelled convenience and availability, companies have a broader set of much more powerful choices through which to interface with the customer. At one point or another, every person in a company, small or large, will interface with the customer, oftentimes without even realizing it. When it comes to the culture key of customer interface, it's very important to remember this. How people feel about the culture of the company they are a part of will directly or indirectly influence its customers. (A quick reminder: A customer includes any person who directly or indirectly is influenced by your product or service.)

Teamwork

More often than not, an individual employee defines culture through their experience with their immediate coworkers, team members, and the leader that they have the most contact with. The study of work-groups and teams in organizations is broad. As a result, there are a great number of definitions and approaches to what we generally refer to as teamwork. The importance of teamwork is obvious. Bring together two or more people, identify a goal for them to accomplish, and you have the basic ingredients of a team. From that foundation it's a matter of scaling it. Without teamwork, things don't get done.

There are three primary approaches to teaming. The first is when the team is organized through a focus on expertise, competencies, and specific areas of specialization. In larger companies, this is also accomplished through the use of approaches to project management or through a matrix structure. These approaches are best served as ad hoc and fluid. A focus on leveraging specific competencies can also result in teams that are focused on a certain content area or type of work, or are organized to perform a particular function of the company.

Another primary approach is that of cross-functional teams. The role definitions for members of cross-functional teams generally require members to act more as generalists than specialists. The key characteristics that are looked for and that align an individual to the team are a willingness to collaborate and build consensus, and place priority on contributing to the performance of the team, and an ability to move in and out of the various roles within the team.

The third primary form of teaming focuses on individual freedom and the alignment of each person's contribution to the central cause or ideals of the team. Often in a hybrid-like fashion, team members can act as generalists as well as specific content specialists. What differs are the motivation of the group and how it is brought to life through the team members. Team members have a great deal of autonomy, and the key characteristic of alignment is whether they demonstrate a commitment to the idealistic values and goals of the whole.

Structure

It is our opinion that when it comes to the structural alignment of a company, structure follows form. All too often leaders and their companies fall into the trappings of past experiences, models, and frameworks for how to build and run companies. The most alluring are organizational and team structure. Maybe because it has been so many times before, our ideas about how to organize and structure companies into functional components requires the least amount of creativity. Perhaps it is because we have the organizational charts, with their many rectangles and lines, burned indelibly into our brains. So much so that perhaps they're encoded in our shared DNA of how organizations should work.

There are two interesting aspects of how many leaders go about designing and structuring their companies. One is that they do it from the inside out. Though this allows for companies to focus on the operational elements of how it creates and delivers a product or service, it often fails to put the most important aspect of the business out in front: the customer. As a result, the organization's structure can end up misaligned to the customer experience, and not agile and responsive enough to the constant changes that customers drive. The second is simply that the design and structure that works for one company will likely not fully align to and serve another company as well.

Aligned Values

This is often one of the keys to success that is given a great deal of attention, but it is also the one that's often more poorly executed on than the others. In fact, when asked, often leaders in organizations are unable to articulate the set of core values that they themselves contributed to creating. Ask a group of people in an organization to all individually write a one-sentence definition for a value, and you'll be surprised at how many different definitions you'll get. The lesson is that it's simply not good enough to hang the words on the wall, post them to your website, or repeat them at company meetings. For people to understand them, and take responsibility for them, requires leaders to talk about them constantly and consistently. It requires leaders to explain what the values mean, what they represent, and how significant they are to the culture of the company.

Furthermore, it requires leaders to relentlessly role-model and reinforce them. The core values of a culture cannot be overstated, overcommunicated, or overly reinforced. It is that important. Values speak to how people treat one other. They speak to what is expected and how the individuals of an organization are intended to work together. When all is said and done, values define the core of culture. They describe the intended human experience.

———

Design thinking changes how people work together and inevitably will influence the culture they work in. By combing the culture keys with design thinking, we see two important mechanisms at work. The first is the influence of several of the attributes of design thinking organizations, including cultural awareness, the right problems, open spaces, co-creation, whole communication, and design thinking at scale. The second are the culture keys and how they are being affected by the attributes of design thinking, including influence, problem-solving, decision-making, conflict management, role definition, teamwork, and customer interface. Understanding how they are applied is an important ingredient to success. In the next chapter, we'll take a closer look at how cultures become the unique creatures they are and how understanding their uniqueness allows for the further leveraging of design thinking in any organization.

5

Culture Types

*"A company's culture is the foundation
for future innovation. An entrepreneur's
job is building the foundation."*
—Brian Chesky

In the last chapter, we introduced you to our definition of culture and provided insight into the culture keys, providing an understanding of the traits and characteristics associated with culture. Now we turn our attention to a key to successfully introducing and implementing design thinking into any organization. The reason we're saying "any" is to bring attention to the vital need to align the process of how design thinking is implemented to the organization's culture. As we mentioned in the previous chapter, every organization has a unique culture. Having a framework for interpreting a culture, and aligning the approach to design thinking's implementation and use, is essential.

In doing the research for this book, we conducted more than 70 in-depth interviews with design leaders and executives from the organizations in our study group, throughout which we focused on the convergence of design thinking, culture, and innovation. Among the design leaders we interviewed was Kevin Lee, a VP and global head of design at Visa. Kevin is at the forefront in the development of Visa's human-centered innovation capabilities, and, over time, is seeing effect and influence of design thinking on its culture. His focus is using design thinking as a way to "create experiences that everyone can relate to."

Kevin is one of those people who is so deeply committed and believes so much in what he is doing and bringing to the world, a conversation with him is getting a glimpse of what it must feel like to be "evangelized and converted into becoming a believer in the power of design thinking." The insight Kevin Lee offers is powerful. It's always about the human experience. It is through the experience that people gain a sense of the environment they are in, and that creates their interpretation and perception of an organization's culture.

This is key to understanding what culture is and how to change, shift, or ultimately transform it. When the experience changes in the environment and in our day-to-day experience, people's perception and understanding of the culture begins to shift. As human beings, experiences create connections to our emotions. When people undergo change, their emotional senses are heightened. They become more aware of the resulting excitement, fear, or even anger that they associate with the change. If the change feels good, people want more of it and naturally look to replicate it. If it doesn't feel good and people have a negative perspective, they deny, resist, and avoid it.

> Eventually, how well an organization adopts and integrates design thinking becomes a matter of engagement.

This has a great deal to do with how design thinking is adopted, integrated, and embedded as way of doing things and attaining success in organizations. Because culture is about the "how-to" of individual and collective success, and what is acceptable and unacceptable, how an organization will integrate and possibly embed design thinking and its elements, as well as to what extent it will influence its culture, can vary. However it starts, how design thinking succeeds and to what ends it results in being an attribute of an organization's future, is dependent on the commitment of leadership and the ability of a culture to shift and change in a manner that evolves into a design thinking culture.

Eventually, how well an organization adopts and integrates design thinking becomes a matter of engagement. The engagement of people's creativity can't be mandated. Kevin Lee refers to the experience at Visa as "a self-sustaining spiral of engagement." The same momentum of engagement, he points out, is also spreading to become a part of Visa's culture. Though not every part of the company and its 11,000 employees will in the near future evolve into the intended culture, an investment in design thinking is spreading out across the company and is, in much of the organization, modifying and shifting the culture. The same can be said for Visa's culture, which is becoming the company's foundation for innovation and the leveraging of its collective imagination. The culture shifts are happening.

CULTURE KNOWLEDGE

As part of our research on culture, we wanted to inquire, compare answers, and synthesize based on a fairly extensive list of questions. In our interviews, although we asked a broad spectrum of questions regarding design thinking and innovation, one of the things we wanted to find out about is the different ways in which design thinking was introduced to and integrated into the various and unique cultures of our study group organizations. Our questions focusing on culture included:

1. How did the use of design thinking get initiated in the organization?
2. How was design thinking implemented and integrated into the organization?
3. How has it influenced the organization's culture?
4. How has it influenced the organization's leadership?
5. How has it influenced decision-making?

What we found is that there are a host of differing approaches to successfully introducing, implementing, and embedding design thinking into an organization. Consistent with the *True Alignment* framework, we were able to test the idea of one size does not fit all and found that the organizations not only had different starts to their use of design thinking, but found that finding and using the right recipe for an organization's unique culture is an important part to being successful. As we outlined in Chapter 2, a set of attributes is common to design thinking organizations. Some may already be present at the start. Others show up and develop as the organization moves further along the path and result in shifts in a culture. That being said, we found there are three key "how-to" ingredients to being successful in the journey.

The first is the ability to recognize and understand the current culture of the organization. Right at the outset, to be successful in bringing any new way of doing things into an organization, it's important to understand how people are presently experiencing the culture in its current form and to have clarity as to what behavioral changes are being sought. Having a thorough appreciation of the current culture also presents the opportunity to create a baseline from which to observe and measure the behavioral change and effect that the integration of design thinking is having.

In assessing the current culture, leaders should make sure the criteria for observation and measurement of change includes the behavioral attributes that are to be influenced. It's a good idea to make sure that the assessment or audit being used covers these important components of culture, as well as any other culture traits that are part of the culture change being sought.

The second important ingredient is to engage your journey of culture change with an open mind. Remember the natural tension between the need for predictability and ambiguity? It's much like GE's Jeff Immelt pointed out when he shared his early impression of the rise of the creative class, saying, "I thought it was a little bit of B.S. initially, I wasn't sure," and his coming to realize that "[i]t is real."[1]

Immelt's view is not only candid and refreshing, it's also very telling. It's important to be open to what the world is telling you and embracing it. When leaders start down the path of culture change, being curious and open to whatever the organization and its culture can become is as liberating as it is true. Let's face it: We never really know what's next. Letting go allows us to see what's available and engage the world of possibility in new ways. And it may not be what you expected.

The third ingredient is the application of the culture keys. As an example, it's important to recognize the value of redefining teamwork and providing the necessary facilitation and leadership coaching, or to explore how people are incented and rewarded. In an expertise culture that applies performance-based pay based on individual achievement, in which people are more concerned with their personal performance, it may require the addition of a form of team recognition, celebration, or reward to influence contribution to a team's outcome and reinforce the more collaborative behaviors required by design thinking.

Along with the other two ingredients of understanding the current culture and openness to the unexpected changes, applying the culture keys to support the integration of design thinking dramatically increases the likelihood for an any organization to succeed in implementing and getting the benefits of design thinking. One of the more powerful aspects of the design thinking experience is the white space it creates for asking, "What's missing?" The use of the culture keys in combination with the culture types provides for a wonderful platform from which to discover and explore how to best engage design thinking in your organization.

FIRST ASSESS, THEN SHIFT, THEN TRANSFORM

In Chapter 3, we introduced you to the concept of the collective imagination and how design thinking leverages the emotional motivation it provides. As a quick reminder, the three pillars of the collective imagination are participation, the pursuit of knowledge, and the freedom of expression.

Recognizing and understanding the three sources of motivation provides us with powerful insight into how design thinking connects to the traits and characteristics of culture, and what makes cultures both similar and as unique as each is. The result is a set of three distinct preferences known as the participation, expertise, and authenticity cultures.[2]

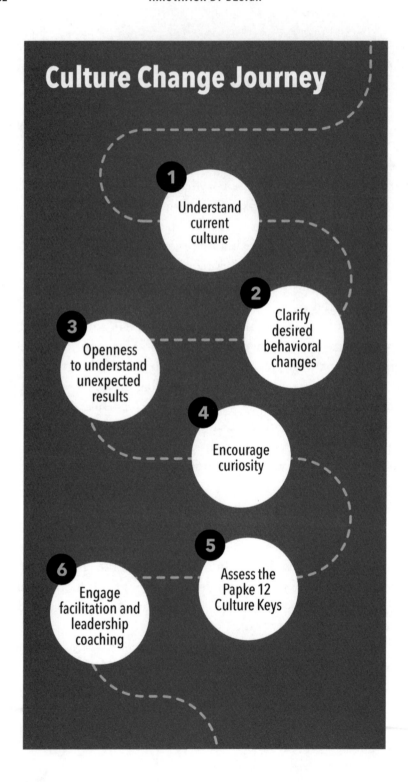

The culture types are much like personality types, providing insight into the key behavioral norms in a culture as well as its unique makeup of the traits and characteristics common to all organizations. From a systems design perspective, applying the three types allows for the intentional design of a culture that best suits the pursuit of an organization, influencing how it can be more successful in the creation and delivery of its product or service to the marketplace, and to compete at higher levels. From the perspective of cultural change and transformation, the platform of the three culture types allows for the assessment of an organization's current culture and provides the identification of the means through which to best introduce and integrate design thinking.

ALIGNING FOR SUCCESS

The platform provided by the three culture types provides the context for the use of design thinking. It provides the means to observe how

an organization can intentionally develop the traits associated with the profile of design thinking employees, such as empathy, integrative thinking, experimentation, and collaboration. These traits also reflect the motivations of a younger and more diverse thinking workforce and the desire to be more included and engaged, and participate at greater levels and that contribute to the pull factor that contributes to the successful use of design thinking.

The "how to" of aligning design thinking applies to all three culture types: participation, expertise, and authenticity. Throughout the chapters and case studies that follow, you will be able to identify examples in which the application of design thinking is used in alignment with an organization's culture and why the one-size-fits-all approaches don't work. The better the alignment, the more effective and the greater the levels of performance design thinking will deliver. For this purpose, we are taking this time to provide descriptions of the three culture preferences.

What to Look For

Before going into the detailed descriptions, here are some important reminders that also act as how-to advice:

1. Remember that every culture is unique. It is important to be able to observe and measure what the traits and characteristics are that make a culture unique and, when implementing and using design thinking, to be aware of how they influence how people participate, collaborate, debate, and take risks.

2. Be on the lookout for subcultures. When one part of the company has a culture preference that is not aligned with the rest of the company, it can easily be at odds with the rest of the company. Among other issues, this can lead to "us versus them," disagreement on the best way to do things, a lack of cooperation, the hoarding of information, and the undermining of collaboration. These and other issues can result in teams and groups within an

organization using design thinking successfully and others rejecting it. Sometimes it's more about the dysfunction of the relationships than the subject (in this case design thinking).

3. A big contributor to the success of any organization is the ongoing effort that leaders make to coach the people they lead. This includes clearly articulating and having an ongoing open and frank conversation about the organization's culture, including talking about its strengths as well as its challenges. Like any worthwhile relationship, it needs to be talked about to be healthy. You can't expect that someone will be a valuable contributor to the bus unless they know what it looks like and how they can individually succeed.

4. Paying attention to the relationship to—and the role of—the customer is another key aspect of interpreting culture. This brings us back to the value of realizing that, in the vast majority of cases, how people treat one another within an organization's culture is how they treat their customers. Therefore, the better aligned the culture is to the organization's brand and customer promise, the greater the likelihood of trust within the organization and with those outside it.

EXPERTISE CULTURES

In an expertise culture, the key motivation of employees is for the employee to become an expert, building his or her capabilities in their discipline or specialty, and being as competent as possible. Delivering a high level of trust in the competency of its product or service is at the core of its relationship to the customer.

Power and influence are derived by achieving one's status as ranking among the best, at the top of one's peer group. The better one performs, the more they are challenged and given the opportunity to advance. Teams are built by assembling a collective of the best talent available.

ALIGNING DESIGN IN **EXPERTISE** CULTURES:

Leverage individual competency
Expertise based, ad hoc teaming
Support analytical processes
Challenge for better and best
Spur competition
Leverage external expertise
Reward conceptual thinking
Leverage status through and for high achievement

In expertise cultures, the term "individual contributor" is often used, conveying the practice of focusing on individual goals and outcomes.

Those who demonstrate the highest level of expertise primarily do the planning and goal-setting. Membership in committees and ad hoc teams is usually earned and typically decided by those with already established competency. For the process of planning and goal-setting for an entire company, functional experts do the work of defining their particular set of goals and plans, and then come together to agree on the company-wide plan and outcomes. Expertise cultures work best when individuals are change champions and teams are change initiators.

When it comes to problem-solving, in an expertise culture, the best and brightest people are relied on to solve problems. This often results in people that are the "go to" resources that enjoy the reputation of creating solutions and answers to the most pressing or difficult problems. When it comes to problem-solving, expertise cultures typically like to engage only the people who need to be involved. For the most part, members of expertise cultures avoid meetings. After all, unless there is a personal benefit, going to meetings is a waste of time and keeps them from getting their work done.

Decision-making is generally top-down or content specific. At best, decisions are left to those with the greatest degree of knowledge, expertise, and know-how. When managing conflict, expertise cultures typically like a good argument. That is, people like to challenge each other's positions, creating an environment that promotes digging deeper into a problem, and applying logic and data to come to the best outcome. An argument is a position based on fact, logic, and sound reasoning, and is not intended to be emotional.

The primary approach to incentive and reward in an expertise culture is individual recognition and reward. This includes the approaches of pay-for-performance, competency-based pay and status, promotion and rank, as well as tying reward to the direct outcomes of the employee's efforts. Individual recognition for one's aptitude and accomplishments are sources of motivation. Hiring in expertise cultures is generally competency focused. The process itself typically reinforces finding and hiring the person with the best skill, knowledge, and aptitude for the job. Quite often the message a newcomer gets is "Welcome. Show us what you can do."

Role definition is highly oriented to the leveraging of abilities, skills, and know-how. For this reason, oftentimes expertise cultures organize into functional areas and teams, thereby allowing for the predictable application of specialties and increased efficiency. Customer interface is generally left to those that demonstrate that specific competency, and most expertise cultures organize functionally to meet the product and service requirements considered to be the most important. The basic principle is to put those that have the highest level of customer management proficiency in roles that best respond to the customer's needs.

Teamwork can best be described as having a functional or project focus. The main emphasis is on bringing together individual competency to leverage group performance. More and more, expertise culture organizations are adapting and applying variations of project, program, and ad hoc teaming. Unplanned and impromptu teaming is an aspect of high-performing companies that generally translates into greater speed, collaboration, information-sharing, and the culture values of agility and empowerment that we so often hear about. Typically, it also results in higher levels of transparency and trust across the different parts of the company. Expertise cultures most often structure in ways that emphasize the coming together of functionality and hierarchy.

The aligned values of expertise cultures often include challenging, expertise, analytical, innovative, excellence, world-class, preeminent, solutions-oriented, leading edge, high-performing, entrepreneurial, fast-paced, unique, mastery, teamwork, professionalism, and personal excellence.

PARTICIPATION CULTURES

"We're all in this together." Participation cultures often refer to themselves as family-like and pride themselves on being inclusive and collaborative, including the level of attention and inclusion of the customer.

Much of the influence that motivates members of the culture comes from a high level of involvement. Power and influence are gained through participation and involvement. Those who are considered most aligned with the culture are typically seen as amiable, friendly, and outgoing. Planning and goal-setting are accomplished through involvement and sharing. Large group processes that involve everyone are most likely to result in success. Problem-solving is a shared process and is teamwork-driven. When someone, or the team, has an issue that needs to be resolved, or a challenge to be confronted, it is best served by getting the team together.

Decision-making is also a shared process that is group-driven. Often, leaders in participation cultures look to the team to make decisions. At the very least, they will typically ask for input from the team. Disagreement generally leads to collaboration and shared problem-solving. Often, a participation culture's members will work toward finding out what outcome best serves the best interest of the team and accommodating a shared point of view. Among the approaches to incentive and reward, those that best align to and reinforce group and team contribution are shared reward, equity, team recognition, and social celebrations. Often, social celebrations will have a greater positive affect than shared monetary rewards.

When it comes to hiring, group involvement in the interviewing and decision-making process are keys to success. Often the primary concern is finding the best team players that offer the best interpersonal fit with the other members of the team. Role definition in the participation culture usually centers on being a team player and the ability to work well with one's fellow teammates. Getting along is important, as is the ability to work cross-functionally. When it comes to development, when a member of the team goes off for training, they are generally expected to share their information and learning with others. Cross-functional teams work directly with the customers they serve and they spend time with them. Through a natural extension of the culture, the customer is often the center of focus or considered "one of us."

Teamwork is all about involvement and looking out for one another, and the communication is informal and free-flowing. More often than not, the structures of participation preference cultures

ALIGNING DESIGN IN **PARTICIPATION** CULTURES:

Leverage participation and involvement
Reinforce cross-functional teaming
Support integrated group processes
Focus on shared rewards and group celebration
Leverage customer focus and partnering
Reward team accountability and contribution
Engage broad involvement

consist of relatively flat hierarchies. To support interaction and informal communication, participation cultures will generally show partiality to open workspaces and environments.

Among others, the core values that participation cultures often use to define their culture include teamwork, sense of family, collaboration, listening, community, respect for the individual, equality, cooperation, fairness, diversity, and inclusiveness.

AUTHENTICITY CULTURES

In authenticity cultures, power and influence are gained by demonstrating a commitment to the values and higher ideals of the organization and its mission. Typically, the goal is to provide the customer with intrinsic value that demonstrates a sense of caring for, and the desire to help them physically and psychologically reach their potential.

Those who interact with others in charismatic and inspiring ways often have the greatest influence. It is not as much about being the best and the brightest or the friendliest, it is about being genuine and authentic and engaging others. Being optimistic and positive, as well as showing compassion and empathy, generally results in the ability to have an effect on others.

Planning and goal-setting are centered on the values and beliefs of what is possible and that which best delivers to the cause. Participation in planning is most often group-based, and there is a sense of community in how people come together to agree on goals. A shared sense of purpose and organic process are not unusual ways for an authenticity culture to strategize. Problem-solving is focused on the intention of the group and often involves open dialogue as to what solutions may work. Subjective and intuitive approaches are considered and are often given as much or more attention than more analytical-based ideas. Group members expect one another to be open to sharing and hearing each other's ideas, thereby promoting creativity and provoking each other to think imaginatively. In an authenticity culture, employees are welcome to contribute insights and ideas, regardless how "out of the box" they may appear to be.

Decision-making is often influenced by ethical and moral considerations and filtering decisions through the lens of whether a decision aligns with what the right thing to do is. How a decision aligns to the core values and beliefs of the group is often more important than its measurable financial or performance outcome. Finding alignment between the two often offers the best alternative. In an authenticity culture, disagreements and conflicts are usually dealt with openly. Individuals will typically be rigid in protecting the company's values and ideals, and its definition of what the right thing to so is, and members of authenticity cultures will often pride themselves on being self-aware and showing flexibility. In the end, outcomes to conflict are generally those that further develop the relationships of those involved, including increased intimacy and trust. A great degree of emphasis is placed on employees being genuine and honest. Open expression of thoughts and feelings are expected. On the other hand, employees that are perceived as disingenuous or withholding will typically find themselves in jeopardy.

In authenticity cultures, incentives and rewards are often intrinsic, and members are more motivated by the purpose and values of the company. Another form of reward that is typical of an authenticity culture is the opportunity for personal development and self-actualization. In light of the greater degree to which the culture honors self-expression and openness, the opportunity for personal growth and the pursuit of one's professional and personal passions are great motivators. Hiring is highly intentional and decisions are primarily made on the basis of how perspective employees connect to the company's purpose and culture. Working with one another means being caring and considerate, and building relationships that are open and honest.

These same qualities show in how authenticity cultures approach role definition. There is a sense of individual empowerment that conveys people to pursue that which best satisfies the immediate fulfillment of the company's purpose. When it comes to customer interface, the same ethos applies: Customers are to be connected with and cared for. In an authenticity culture, this means that, regardless of an employee's position or role, everyone is empowered to provide service. Teamwork comes fairly naturally to authenticity cultures. The key motivation for teamwork is the shared ideals and values of the team's members. Individual teams are often empowered to take responsibility for their own planning and goal-setting. Among others, the aligned values that are common to authenticity cultures include inspiring, values-driven, caring, values-centered, integrity, truth, transparency, generosity, creative, uplifting, self-expression, actualizing, spirituality, positive, realizing, optimistic, faith, and love.

Among the other characteristics to consider in defining the three culture types are meetings, performance management practices, employee time off and leave policy, what people wear, employee discipline, use of information technology, and the processes and tools that are used in measuring, reporting, and assessing performance results. The key is to always consider how these and other factors contribute to and influence the experiences of all those involved, including the customer.

ALIGNING DESIGN IN **AUTHENTICITY** CULTURES:
Encourage personal self-actualization
Leverage group empowerment
Reinforce the higher ideal
Explore the intuitive
Trust in the organic process
Remind that emotion and meaning matter
Focus on openness and trust
Let people play and be creative

Before we move to the next chapter, we thought it would be useful to note that a majority of the organizations in our study group are expertise cultures. It has been our experience that in light of their size and requirements to organize, for many organizations this is a natural outcome. Not all of the organizations that make up our study group have expertise type cultures. Among those that do, they are all unique and there are differences among them. Again and again, we are reminded that when it comes to culture, one size fits all doesn't apply. And, that every organization has a unique culture and that anything is possible.

Out of curiosity, we also did a review of the clients that we worked with over the past 15 years. Keeping in mind that every organization has a unique culture of its own, we found that when it comes to type—from early-stage startups to large, multinational organizations across many industries, and inclusive of profit, not-for-profit, and social entities—more than 70 percent of the organizations that we have engaged have expertise cultures.

There are two conclusions we draw from this data. First, historically, in light of the quest of human beings to organize and create predictability and efficiency, we have naturally found the form of expertise cultures to be the most attractive and likely perceive it to be—despite its potential drawbacks—the most reliable and easiest to manifest management control in. Second, design thinking offers a systemic means through which to overcome many of its drawbacks and increase engagement in the creative process. Design thinking helps to manifest the interdisciplinary and cross-functional collaboration and engagement required to create the necessary change and deliver greater levels of expertise in innovation.

In the next part of this book, we move from laying the foundation for how culture, innovation, and design thinking come together, to exploring the attributes of design thinking organizations and their cultures. Before you turn to the next chapter, we invite you to take some time to explore your organization's culture and find the uniqueness that it offers. By doing so, not only will you be better equipped to understand how the attributes fit, you'll also discover how design thinking can be used to elevate and leverage any organization's uniqueness to help it be more innovative.

The following summary is intended to help you in your exploration.

	EXPERTISE	PARTICIPATION	AUTHENTICITY
Power and Influence	Individual competency and skills, expertise, authority, ranking	Participation, inclusion, affiliation, involvement, importance	Demonstrating commitment to higher ideals, inspiring, affection, openness, optimism
Role Definition	Competency and expertise-driven, "individual contributor," functional role	Team player, cross-functional, group process, information-sharing	Personal growth, empowerment, self-actualizing, personal interest, values-driven
Planning and Goal-Setting	Functional, expertise-driven, competency- and knowledge-focused	Group planning, bottom-up, brainstorming, shared planning approaches, common interest	Value-centered, possibility-focused, organic, personal and group empowerment
Problem-Solving	Analytical, efficiency- and effectiveness-driven, functional expertise, reliance on best and brightest	Shared process, participation, "We're all in this together," brainstorming, involve everyone	Intentional, open dialogue, provoking creativity and imagination, possibility focused

	EXPERTISE	PARTICIPATION	AUTHENTICITY
Decision-Making	Top-down or content-driven, single-person or small group	Group-driven process, consensus building, high involvement, collaboration-driven	Ethical, moral-driven, open dialogue, subjective and qualitative, intuitive, empowerment
Reward, Compensation, and Celebration	Meritocratic, status and rank, competition-based, individual contribution	Group, shared reward, "all for one, one for all," equity, social celebration	Intrinsic, meaningful, development-oriented, emotional, peer-related
Customer Interface	Specific competency efficiency-driven, functional, efficient, delivery of expertise and problem-solving	Relationship-based, team interface, customer is "one of us," connection	Personal empowerment, trust, customers are cared for, ideal-related
Hiring	Competency-focused, follow policy and procedure, experts hire experts, job aptitude	Group interview and hiring, focus on interpersonal fit, team-player skills	Highly intentional, connectivity to purpose, values- and belief-driven, honesty

	EXPERTISE	PARTICIPATION	AUTHENTICITY
Conflict Management	Fact- and logic-based, good argument, data-driven, authority-oriented	Consensus-driven, collaborative, shared problem-solving, group interest	Openness, ethics, values-driven, possibility focus, personal and group awareness, intimacy
Aligned Values and Motivations	Challenging, being best, accountability, solutions-focused, role status, quality, competency, entrepreneurial	Teamwork, family, listening, community, inclusiveness, collaboration, cooperation, belonging	Intention, affection, openness, accountability to values and beliefs, idealistic pursuit, actualizing, values-driven
Structure	Hierarchy, functional grouping, efficiency-focused, leverage competency	Relatively flat, cross-functional, team-oriented, connected, shared leadership	Individual empowerment, fluid, organic
Teamwork	Functional, project- or program-focused, ad hoc, intentional, expertise-driven team-player roles	Involvement, looking out for one another, cross-functional, information-sharing	Natural, organic, shared ideals, individual and group empowerment

10 Attributes

6

Design Thinking at Scale

"Design thinking is the glue between all disciplines."
—Arne van Oosterom

We entered our study using criteria that all the organizations, in one form or another, are using design thinking as the methodology of innovation, customer experience, execution, and performance. This includes an interest in finding out how each organization introduced and implemented design thinking as well as how they further integrated and scaled its use. As a result, we found a number of common practices, as well as the uniqueness that accompanied each organization's journey.

One important finding is that innovative design thinking organizations all share the attribute of scaling, an expansion in the use of design thinking throughout their organizations. Regardless of the size of their organization, they see design thinking as a key strategic element of innovation and a means through which to influence their cultures. Through our interviews, we learned that several have integrated design thinking into their organizations with the goal of having every member, in some way, trained in design thinking.

The big lesson is that any organization, of any size, can use design thinking as a means to influence culture and achieve greater levels of innovation. Regardless of size, whether it is 20 people or 300,000, the more people know about how to engage in design thinking, the greater the level of innovation.

Among our group of innovators, the scale of adoption and use varied, as did the manner in which they implemented and integrated it. For some it started with the CEO and was top-down; for others it was bottom-up or has a grassroots origin. Or it came in from the side, finding its way into the organization through a specific function, group, or acquisition, and spreading from there.

What we didn't expect was the scale to which some of the companies and organizations are applying design thinking. As an example, at Intuit, through its acclaimed Design for Delight (D4D) approach, virtually every one of its close to 10,000 employees is trained in design thinking. In our list of study group companies, the numbers are impressive: Kaiser Permanente, 15,000; GE Healthcare, 6,000; Marriott, 5,000; Honeywell, 3,000; and P&G, 1,300. Deutsche Telekom trained over 5,500 in design thinking in 2016 alone. In the span of 2015 to 2017, SAP trained more than 20,000. This clearly explains their capability to innovate and respond to customer needs.

We found that the number of people trained is not only a reflection of the commitment of the organization to increase its capability to solve problems and innovate, it is also a reflection of their understanding of the influence that design thinking will have on its culture, and how each strives to align its culture and leadership to be innovative.

UNIQUE PATHS

How did they do it? The truth of the matter is that each of the organizations in our study group found its own path. Some set a strategic agenda, some just leveraged what they had and grew organically, some relied on outside experts, some recruited executive-level design

COMPANY	NUMBER OF EMPLOYEES TRAINED IN DESIGN THINKING*	HOW HIGH THE TRAINING REACHES
AMP	700	CEO, executive team, open enrollment
AUTODESK	1,000	CEO, executive team, open enrollment
DEUTCHE TELEKOM	8,000	CEO, executive team, and mandatory
GE HEALTHCARE	6,000	Executives, open enrollment, customers
HONEYWELL	3,000	Business unit
IBM	50,000	CEO, top 100 executives, open enrollment
INTUIT	8,000 (100% of company)	CEO, core training for all
J&J	700 (the target in 2018 is 20,000)	Executives, business unit, open enrollment
KAISER PERMANENTE	15,000	Unit levels
MARRIOTT	5,000	CEO, staff, customers
NEW ZEALAND TRADE AND ENTERPRISE	1,000	CEO, executive team, customers, new employee orientation
PROCTER & GAMBLE	1,300	CEO, executive team, open enrollment
PHILIPS	5,000	Executives, staff, customers
SAP	20,000	CEO, executive team, open enrollment
TATA	10,000	Business unit
VISA	1,400 (10% of company)	Executives, open enrollment, customers
WELLS FARGO	400	Executives, open enrollment
YAHOO	6,000	Business units

*Training is ongoing and ever increasing, and some numbers are estimates from the companies, but this gives a general indication of the scale as of May 2017.

leaders, a few acquired design or design thinking firms, some top executives got turned on and cascaded it out, some went through HR, and some just let passionate design thinking employees emerge and spread influence by success. At Marriott and Kaiser Permanente, design thinking started out as function and found its way to becoming a means through which to engage employees in small groups and eventually on a much larger scale. In others, like GE, Philips, Visa, and IBM, organizations invested in the acquisition of talent and strategically developed design thinking as a competency.

Intuit, SAP, Deutsche Telekom, and P&G approached it from the top down. A CEO or leader experienced the power of design thinking and found it to deliver a means through which to solve the most difficult of problems. In other organizations it started as means to which to solve a particular business problem in one part of the organization, and people were naturally drawn to its qualities and wanted in on the game. What was consistent is that, regardless of how it was happening—how it was introduced, implemented, and integrated—people are drawn to participating in design thinking.

We found a number of significant insights as to how organizations come to implement and eventually arrive at embedding design thinking. We also found that as much as an organization's culture is unique, so is its approach to introducing, implementing, and eventually embedding design thinking in their organizations. Furthermore, in light of unique cultural and leadership preferences, the role modeling, reinforcement, and reputation of leaders of how design thinking is used and supported has a great deal to do with both its immediate as well as its longer-term value to an organization.

We identified the early CEO adopters—leaders like A.G. Lafley at P&G, Intuit founder Scott Cook, and SAP founder Hasso Plattner—and found that each had an experience or introduction to design thinking from which they came away with one simple understanding: It is the means through which to solve problems faster and better, and drive innovation through their companies. They all recognized the power of human-centered design as not only the instigator of the innovation they sought in the design and creation of products and services. They also recognized its application to any problem that their organizations would face. Whether at the intuitive or intellectual level, they experienced and saw potential of the pull factor and leveraging of the collective imagination.

COMMITMENT INFLUENCES CULTURE

Organizations took different paths, but it is clear that design thinking is critical to influencing their cultures to be more innovative. And each goes about it in a unique way, reflecting both the culture when they started, how it has shifted and, in some cases, transformed along the way. How they got there is as individual and unique as their cultures. Along with these findings, we also came away with a set of conclusions that are important to the success that each has created. The conclusions include:

In PwC's 2016 report of *The Global Innovation 1000 Study*, in the ranking of the top innovators and spenders, of the 10 most innovative companies, only half are on the list of the top 20 R&D spenders.[1]

- Scaling matters. Leadership knows how important it is to provide design thinking skills and give access to design thinking to its workforce, and understands the significance of being able to apply design thinking to all parts of the organization, or as many as possible.
- It's not always about spending money on big training programs. What is important is to identify and hire people with the right mindset and get them out in the organization coaching and training people by engaging them in doing. Regardless of who they are and where they work in the organization, it's about teaching them to think like (some) designers, or better-stated design thinkers, including role-modeling what it looks like.
- Naming or branding a design thinking program helps uniquely align the effort to the company and elevate the importance of its application and use, and provides

a common language and framework. It communicates that it is more than just worthwhile doing, and not just a department thing. It signals the importance of participating and what it represents to the culture. And, it provides a way for users to associate and identify with its value and becomes a source of pride. That said, unique names could also cause confusion. About half of the sample group just called it Design Thinking, which also makes sense.

- Leadership involvement is powerful. Eventually, if leaders aren't versed in design thinking and don't learn to get out of peoples' way to use it, it can undermine everything an organization is setting out to accomplish. The best leaders of design thinking are those who are curious and practice it themselves.

- There is no one roadmap that every organization has to follow to get to the promised land of creating an innovative design thinking culture. The path will be unique. This requires leaders to be adaptable and aware of the path as it unfolds and not to be constrained by holding on to what the culture has been in the past. Rather, to think like a designer, adapt to the user needs and keep an eye out for what's missing and the culture needs most.

- The passion and creativity of design thinkers are something to embrace. They embed design thinking into the culture with the goal of shifting mindset and making it part of the organization's DNA. They commit to the idea of creating human-centered cultures and leveraging design thinking to inspire cultures of innovation.

Reinforcing what we stated at the outset of this chapter, among our key findings, the most important is the understanding that any organization can leverage design thinking to become a more innovative culture. This is proven through the fact that, though there are similarities in how some of the organizations in our study group have introduced and integrated design thinking, each has a unique story to tell.

For some, at the early-stage development of the organization and culture, it provided an immediate engine for creativity and growth. For other, more mature organizations, it became a beacon for change and cultural transformation, inviting shifts in mindset and in long-standing beliefs and behaviors. In several cases, their story becomes a part of the organization's history and lore, which is known to people inside and outside the organization. It also becomes a key influence on not only the culture, but it also extends to the customer experience and interactions with all its stakeholders. Design thinking also becomes a great source of pride.

DNA BY DESIGN

A little more than a decade ago, long before Intuit began thinking of itself as a design-driven company with the desire to embed design thinking in its DNA, it began its journey in what is now an amazing tale of transformation that is a cornerstone of its story and culture. The story anchors a set of initial shifts in its culture that produced the design thinking scaling effort the company set out on—and, so far, it has succeeded in very well.

In about 2006, Intuit's founder, Scott Cook, recognized that Intuit had to become more innovative and decided to encourage all employees to spend 10 percent of their time on unstructured projects. His inspiration came from Google's 20-percent unstructured time model. Being that Intuit is an accounting software company, Cook thought that 10 percent seemed more prudent. Shortly thereafter, he was further inspired by an article about design thinking written by Roger Martin at Rotman University in Toronto. Design thinking had been a method of problem solving used by designers for many years, and now a business school was suddenly getting press about its application as a creative way to solve business problems by thinking like a designer. Cook learned it was about using abductive reasoning for problem-solving, versus deductive or inductive reasoning. As he absorbed more about design thinking, he wondered whether it could help his accounting software company be more innovative. Concurrent with his pursuits and increasing knowledge about design thinking came the company's realization that, as the 10 percent of unstructured time initiative moved on, Intuit employees didn't know how to spend the time well.

In 2007, to reinvigorate Inuit's performance, Cook and then-CEO Steve Bennett decided to focus on the role of design in the company. Cook created a one-day program he called Design for Delight (D4D) and, with the intention of setting out on a transformation toward being a design-driven company, invited the company's top 300 managers to an off-site meeting. Based on deep customer empathy, idea generation, and experimentation, D4D was created to clearly articulate Intuit's approach to design thinking and to provide the entire company with a common framework for building great products. Cook then delivered a five-hour PowerPoint presentation to which he received a polite, yet unengaged response.[2]

For the offsite, Cook also invited Alex Kazaks, an associate professor from Stanford, to present for an hour. Kazaks took a different approach to his segment: Rather than present from a PowerPoint, he engaged the audience in a design thinking experience including prototyping, feedback, iterating, and refining. When asked, two-thirds of the off-site participants provided the feedback that most of what they learned occurred in Kazaks one-hour presentation and the hands-on activity. When Cook understood the significance of the moment, he decided that shift in Intuit's culture was badly needed. This prompted what has become the journey of Intuit toward embedding design thinking into the company's culture—its DNA.[3]

When Thomas was president of the Design Management Institute, part of his role was the oversight of all content and programming for DMI, which included developing three conferences per year (in the United States, Europe, and Asia); during his six-year tenure he produced 22 conferences for design leaders. Thomas decided to run the 2009 U.S. conference in San Francisco and invited Roger Martin and Darrel Rhea to join him as co-chairs. They called it Re-Thinking Design and invited Scott Cook to be a speaker. It was one of the first conferences about design thinking, and the first time DMI had a CEO speak at a conference. As much as Scott had a great impact on the audience, the conference and its passionate design leaders in attendance also had inspired him.

This may have led to the second step in Intuit's design thinking journey: the development of a team of design thinking coaches. The team consisted of aptly named "Innovation Catalysts," whose role was to work with managers throughout the company in their product initiatives. The idea is not to offer the direct expertise to solve a problem, but rather, to offer managers and teams the means through which to apply design thinking. Over the past decade, more than 1,500 Innovation Catalysts have been trained, and taken three, five, or 14 days of design thinking leadership training. The training is all done internally, employee to employee.

The Innovation Catalyst idea came from early benchmarking with P&G. The key was selecting people interested in design thinking to become catalysts, not just because they were skilled at it, but rather because they also have a passion for it and, in their words, "can turn the lights on" for other people and unleash their creativity. Many of the company's Innovation Catalysts are not even in what would be considered as creative roles (accountants, for example). The company's key discovery is that design thinking is not about the roles and jobs that people do; rather it's about people, and their interest to collaborate, to be creative, to participate, to seek to understand, to have empathy, and to create solutions, regardless of the role participants are in. And it's about the unexpected results that come with it.

As an example, a group that primarily focuses on TurboTax, and is very product- and feature-driven, is always looking for insights and inspiration into the not-so-inspirational watching of how people do tax returns. To use their creative time, they often explore how to make improvements in the way products are sold. During a two-day design thinking workshop, one team had taken on an experiment that failed and needed a new problem to fill their remaining time. One of the team members raised the question as to why the product they were working on was only sold in seats of five and not in single seats. They concluded that perhaps someone in product management, at one point in time, thought that selling multiple seats was the optimal way to sell. To test their idea, the team suggested changes to the script used in the call center. They then ran some quick tests right then, on the fly, with call center staff, customers, and prospects. In a very short period of time they learned that many more people were interested in buying just one seat, or three seats. As a result, after further testing, they changed their policy to sell individual and smaller numbers of seats. What was the result of this small customer-centric, quick prototype test? A $10 million increase in sales in the first year.

In another example, Intuit's finance organization recognized that 25 percent of their customers didn't update their credit cards in time and were cut off from service. They questioned why customers did not respond to their emails in advance of the expiration date. After some contextual research with customers, and through the use of some open-ended questions, they soon discovered that in about 25 percent of the small businesses using QuickBooks, Intuit's emails were not finding the right person. Unfortunately, from the customer's point of view, suddenly one day QuickBooks stopped working and left them feeling frustrated or angered at the company. The group ran a series of small experiments on how to keep contact information up to date and to find better ways to communicate with their customers. The company estimates recovering approximately $8 million a year in lost revenue, simply by improving communication and engagement with customers in keeping billing information up to date.

To further embed design thinking into the culture DNA, the company organized a series of D4D forums, which were attended by more than 1,000 employees each. At the forums, employees heard success stories, listened to experts talk about design and design thinking, and were asked at a personal level to initiate change in how they did their jobs. In other words, the company was asking every employee to apply design thinking to their individual roles in the company.

When it comes to scaling design thinking through an organization, one of the key factors consistent among our study group is the importance of executives to be trained and in support of it. Another key step in Intuit's journey (to present day) was the integration of design thinking into its approach to leadership development. This meant not just exposing them to design thinking and getting the help of catalysts, but rather, leaders learned to directly apply design thinking to how they and their teams solved problems. There's evidence of the influence of design at the executive ranks as well. In 2006 Intuit had six designers in positions at the executive level. By 2016, that number had increased to 35.

A few years ago the company realized that, as new executive leaders joined the company, they began to have more untrained executives. Knowing that design thinking had to be internalized, they began asking executives when they last visited a customer. Upon realizing the gap that existed, they set an agenda for every employee, at the director level and above, to go out 12 times a year with customers and other experts to try to develop new ideas and develop a point of view about the future. Recently, the company held an event involving the top 400 people in the company. Each person had to share their personal vision and, based on customer input, deliver new ideas for innovating in the future. Now being integrated as part of employee performance reviews, once a month, the top 400 people in the company have to demonstrate their plans for innovation that contributes to the delivery of a customer benefit. At Intuit, the approach is to consider design thinking as a core competency for everyone.

Today, Intuit's design thinking group, called the Innovation Capabilities Team, reports to the chief of staff in the office of the president. Having design thinking report directly into the office of the president, Brad Smith, is powerful evidence of the company's continuing commitment to design thinking.[4] The commitment that started with its founder, Scott Cook, not only carries on with the new CEO, it is enhanced. This is because it works, and because the leadership at Intuit is aligned around the power of design thinking.

THE HOW-TO OF INTUIT'S SUCCESS

If you're thinking about what the culture type Inuit is, it is expertise. What started as a journey to bring design thinking into Intuit has provided a powerful case study for transforming an expertise culture from one that relied on scientific methods and the intellectual pursuit of innovation—long planning periods, approval-gathering prior to prototyping, meetings reviewing PowerPoint decks, slow decision-making, arguing over whose ideas are better, competing for resources, developers writing code for months on end only to have specs change—to one that is action oriented through energetic engagement and doing things together. The aforementioned traits, ranging from long planning periods to competition of resources, are common to behaviors we typically associate with expertise cultures that have not discovered the need to integrate greater levels of collaboration and teamwork. Through their strictly intellectual pursuit, they likely have not developed the communication and teaming skills associated with empathy, listening, and collaborative problem-solving.

Now, the way Intuit strives to work relies on engineers, designers, marketers, and product managers all interfacing with their customers to develop empathy for the customer and their experience, thereby focusing on the design of solutions. Wendy Castleman, Intuit's design innovation coach and thought leader, explains that being successful calls for a clearly communicated framework for people working together that needs to be taught to everyone. She describes her dream this way: "I hope design thinking as a whole new way of problem solving is here forever." She stresses the need for new areas and disciplines, because design thinking is not about occupations, it's about people and solutions. One of the key learning outcomes at Intuit is that for it to further transform from being a design thinking culture to a design doing culture requires everyone to understand design and apply design thinking.

In an interview at the 2016 O'Reilly Design Conference, Susan Pelican of Intuit shared the need for the nine-year journey as being necessary for Intuit to ready itself for the future. She talked about three stages that the company went through. The first was in 2007, when the company began setting its sights back on focusing on the customer and its need to innovate. She points out that some 30 years prior, the company started with a customer focus and over time evolved into a technology company. It had to refocus and get back to being a more customer-focused organization.[5]

The second stage was creating a culture of innovation. Accomplishing it required the development and engagement of every employee. That meant investing in the training of every member of the company so that they could effectively engage and participate in the application of design thinking. That design thinking would be embedded in the organization's DNA—its culture.

The third stage of the transformation, some nine years from when it was started 2007, is focusing all the effort of the last decade to creating amazing experiences for customers in a quickly shifting landscape and marketplace, and responding to the massive shift in the customer experience. This requires the work of the nine-year journey of developing the entire employee base, the company's expertise culture to operate in a new, more focused way.

Before moving forward, let's conduct a quick review of Intuit's journey to become a design-driven organization. It makes for a great list of how-tos for achieving success in the scaling of design thinking:

- Leadership is deeply committed and involved. The introduction to design thinking was made by the company's founder, Scott Cook, and then-CEO Steve Bennett. Along with leadership development, the increase from having six designers in executive roles in 2007, to nine years later having 35 is a good indication of the strategy to have human-centered design as a critical leadership competency.
- By providing innovation catalysts, the company provides support and the further development of design thinking as a company-wide skill set. It was about going out and doing it.
- Intuit committed itself to training its workforce and leverage its design thinking program. The company invested the time and energy through training all of its employees, regardless of their role in the company.
- Intuit developed an identity and brand for its program. D4D is deeply embedded in the company's culture and is

also becoming a source of great pride (as well as a good
recruiting tool).

- They work at getting everyone on the bus (every
employee trained in design thinking) and giving them
the experience of design thinking and how to achieve
greater levels of collaboration and success. This includes
the company's Innovation Forums, which are attended
by more than 1,000 employees.
- The company provides a clear definition and communication of the organization's intended culture.
- There is a vision for the future of Intuit and giving the
desired transformation a name (a "design doing" culture).
- The company started its journey without a clear roadmap. As Suzanne Pelican points out, the nine-year
journey to get the company and its culture to the present
state was more about purpose and creation of a design-
driven organization and then becoming a design thinking one. It's much less about having a roadmap as it is
unfolding and recognizing the next step in the change
process and what's missing and needed to get there.

ALIGNING LANGUAGE

SAP is the world leader in enterprise applications in terms of software
and software-related service revenue. Based on market capitalization,
the company is the world's third-largest independent software manu-
facturer. Founded by five entrepreneurial programmers in 1972, SAP
has a 45-year history of business innovation and helping the world
run better. Their operational capability and measure of influence are
extraordinary. Worldwide they employ more than 84,000 people and
operate in 130 countries, including more than 100 innovation and
development centers.

It's hard not to come in contact, in some shape or form, with an
SAP software product. The measurement of their commercial success
includes serving 345,000 customer organizations in 180 countries.
Eighty-seven percent of Forbes Global 2000 are SAP customers, and

they have more than 110 million subscribers in their cloud user base. There are more than 15,000 SAP partner companies that are a part of the company's worldwide innovation ecosystem.[6]

As we noted, SAP has trained approximately 20,000 employees in design thinking. Yet, as much as design thinking is integrated into the business, it still has its challenges. One reason is that the term design thinking, inside SAP, has some preconceptions attached to it. Much like any other method that is perceived as a management tool, people associate their connection to it through their own set of experiences. Over time, how it is used and whether it is a good or bad experience influence how individuals and groups relate to it. This is a great reminder that it is always about the experience and the resulting human emotion that affect how motivated people are to use a methodology, regardless how much they are told it will benefit them.

The solution: At SAP, the formula for applying design thinking is *problem finding* × *problem-solving*. Because SAP has such a long history with design and design thinking, the way to overcome any negative baggage associated with design thinking is to stress that innovation and customer empathy are ways of problem-solving, and keeping the focus on solving the right problem. Some would call it creative problem-solving, but it's really more about finding the right problems to solve. To that effect and to create greater clarity, the SAP mindset is to focus design thinking methodology on "problem finding" and viewing design thinking as the means through which to have the ability to scale creativity.

SCALING LEADERSHIP

The story of how design thinking was introduced to and then scaled by SAP is similar to that of Intuit's. Both have story lines in which the main characters are founders. At Intuit it was Scott Cook. At SAP the main character in the story is founder Hasso Plattner. Both leaders recognized that the companies had drifted away from a focus on their customers. And, that there was a need to focus innovation back on the customer experience. Much like Scott's delivery of D4D in 2007, three years before, in 2004, Plattner made an important keynote speech at

Sapphire, their annual sales and marketing meeting with customers, in which he committed the company would get back to its roots with a dedication to what the customers and the end user's need. He challenged the whole company to get back in touch with its DNA and become closer to its customers.

Plattner firmly believed in the power of design thinking for all, and in bringing design thinking into SAP, he essentially wanted to be a company like an in-house design firm, an IDEO. In the time frame of 2004 to 2005, the company built a business case to do just that: a vision for the creation of a design and design thinking culture, which the company's board approved in 2005. The next step was the formation of a design services team, and the company brought on an executive director of design, Sam Yen. Sam had recently obtained a PhD in design theory and methodology from Stanford and turned out to be an excellent fit. The rest is SAP history. From there, the company's design thinking program took hold and was integrated throughout the company and its culture.

To scale design thinking throughout the company, SAP sends its executives to the design thinking boot camp in the d.school to learn about the skill sets of design thinking. One of the few drawbacks of the d.school's program is that it doesn't teach how to build a culture of innovation. Therefore, it relies on the ability of SAP's leadership to assure that the traits associated with design thinking manifest throughout the company's culture. For SAP, this was the next big challenge: the dilemma of how to bring the methodologies of design thinking in-house to build a culture of innovation. It simply relied on the development of the design thinking as a key core competency.

Through this experience, and over the past 13 years, the company has learned a lot about the effects of design thinking, applying it as the core methodology to change its internal processes, for the development of products, and in the understanding of and creating the experiences of customers. It's now a given in the SAP culture. At SAP one simply applies design thinking training in everything you do.

At this point, you're likely able to recognize that as an expertise-type culture, many of the same elements of SAP's design thinking journey are very similar to the journey of Intuit. They include the culture's integration of design thinking as a core competency that reinforces individual and collective expertise; a common language and approach to its use and giving it a common language ("problem finding"); getting executives trained in design thinking and creating an experience that aligns to its desired leadership behavior; clearly articulating the company's culture; and creating a vision and using clear language to communicate it: design thinking in everything they do.

> More than half of the organizations in our study group have CEOs that have participated in design thinking training and workshops. All of the companies have senior executives that have participated.

Before moving on from this chapter, there are two other factors worth mentioning. The first is the power of a meaningful purpose or mission. It provides a framing and motivational encourager for an organization's people. Whereas we give attention to the attribute of purpose in another chapter of the book, we thought it important to recognize here. After all, the intention behind investing time, energy, and financial resources into embedding design thinking into an organization is important. The intention is the organization's purpose.

The second relates to the roles of the CEO and leaders. Every story has a main character. And every story comes to life around a set of characters, actors, and, in the case of the Hunger Project, animators and investors. In the cases of Intuit and SAP, the main characters are Scott Cook and Hasso Plattner. Of the organizations in our study, more than half of their CEOs have undergone training in design thinking. Several have attended Stanford's d.school Design Thinking Bootcamp, and several have taken their executive teams with them. That's just the beginning. The other players in the story include the multitudes of employees and stakeholders involved in the success of their companies. Design thinking at scale isn't much of an option. To leaders and organizations in creating an innovative culture, it's more of a necessity.

7

The Pull Factor

*"Listening is a magnetic and strange thing, a creative
force. When we really listen to people there is an
alternating current, and it recharges us so that we never
get tired of each other. We are constantly re-created."*
—Brenda Ueland

As we see throughout the cases and examples in this book, people
appear to naturally want to engage in design thinking, in part
because their colleagues are. People strive for inclusion. It's what training organization Luma Institute has observed as well; design thinking
initiatives often start with just a few people, and then a few more, and
soon, a community ground swell begins to develop. It can emerge from
the top down, or from the bottom up. People who are trained in design
thinking just tend to lean in, to have fun, to feel engaged and empowered; design thinking democratizes the voice. It's actually rather conta-
gious, because it's such a natural, yet radical, way of problem-solving.
Perhaps, as Amy Hedrick, executive director of the Luma Institute,
pointed out to us, design thinking has the ability to amplify, because

it engages our hearts, our minds, and our hands—our hearts to empathize, our minds to understand, and our hands to create. People love design thinking, because they become empowered to act.

Through our research we discovered that one of the essential traits of innovative cultures is what we named the "pull factor." It is the emotional momentum that results from the natural consequence of people wanting to engage and be part of innovation and the design thinking experience. Equally important, the pull factor power we discovered is driven by all employee generations: Generation Z/iGeneration, Generation Y/Millennials, Generation X, and Baby Boomers.

Our research indicates that design thinking companies embrace the pull factor as a means to innovation. It differs significantly from the more traditional ways in which organizations have viewed engaging members and driving innovation. Many companies have invested boatloads of money in innovation over the years, but smart companies—the design thinking companies—are rethinking how, when, and where they spend money. Rather than continuing to pour small fortunes into, or in addition to, scientific methods and technology innovation, they are investing relatively minimal funding into company-wide design thinking. The reality: Scaling employee creativity by providing design thinking training is both extremely inexpensive and extremely effective. One of the key factors and deliberate priorities of any organization's success in the implementation of a strategy is demonstrated by its commitment of two key resources: time and money. This is particularly true as it relates to the implementation of strategies and methods designed to increase its ability to innovate.

The organizations in this research see design thinking as a means to focus on and develop innovation through which they intend to create their futures. They commit time and money, thereby showing the willingness to invest in its development and application. Though the attributes of this competency are generally seen as a set of softer teamwork skills, they are also recognized as the most challenging for organizations and their employees to manifest and develop. These include the need for open dialogue, sharing ideas, challenging and being challenged, and allowing bigger ideas to emerge. Unfortunately, these are skills that are unlikely to be imparted in traditional business offerings (engineering, science, or management education), where in most cases analytical and scientific methods of problem-solving are taught. The companies in our research show an understanding of the need to invest time and money in the development of these key interpersonal communication skills. This includes the training of design thinking facilitators and practitioners, executive training, team development, and the formation and support of design thinking communities of practice.

A GLOBAL ECOSYSTEM

How do you engage more than 130,000 employees worldwide to think creatively and directly impact the day-to-day customer experience? How do you involve a half-million people in an organization's global ecosystem to engage in design thinking? How do you get them to realize that all their relationships to one another, and their customer, are interdependent, are closely connected, and will bring value to their individual and collective performance?

At first glance, the challenge we are describing is monumental: to engage a worldwide ecosystem that includes more than 500,000 people and scale design thinking to the level of making it available to all of them. It goes well beyond merely implementing a set of processes and systemic applications. Not only does it require thinking and acting much differently at the leadership level, it requires creating a culture that motivates its members and opens them to see design thinking and creative problem-solving as more than just requirements and work processes—but rather, that design thinking is accepted as the true differentiator that everyone, regardless of role, level, or location, believes in. That every member of the organization comes to embrace design thinking for what it represents: a source of creativity that leads to higher levels of engagement and performance.

Getting a half-million people to think this way presents a daunting, if not impossible, mission. Yet, this is the challenge that resulted in the cultural change efforts coming about as the consequence of Marriott International's newly discovered penchant for co-creation.

This desire has resulted in the organization becoming one of the more innovative companies in the world. Still, the accolades of being highly innovative don't begin to give credit to all the performance outcomes the company has manifested over the past several years. The company's financial results speak for themselves.

Over a five-year period from 2011 to 2016, the company generated a 22.3-percent return on shares (compared to an industry average of 16.6 percent),[1] all while expanding and growing at a rapid rate. As a result of its 2016 acquisition of Starwood, Marriott increased its portfolio from 19 to 29 brands. To get a better sense of its performance, prior to the acquisition, in the five-year period from 2011 to 2016, it expanded its presence from 73 countries and territories to 87.[2] And, in the same period, it grew from 3,700 to 4,400 locations worldwide. In 2017, *Forbes* placed it at number five on the list of the world's largest companies.[3]

It would be an over-simplification to credit Marriott's growth and financial results to its acquisition and growth strategies. The true force of the company's success is its ability to innovate and consistently deliver to its customers in new and ingenious ways. It's also one of the ways in which it can be better integrate and leverage the culture of its newly acquired portfolio. Examples of its list of impactful innovations include:

- A mobile app that allows guests to not only check in and out through smartphones and tablets, but also to be used as mobile room keys. The app also provides a handy communication device allowing customers to make specific requests and chat with hotel service providers before, during, and after their stays. Guests can use it for setting wake-up calls, requesting toiletries, and other services.
- Larger and more inviting spaces for guests to interact, offering a community feel to its shared spaces and public areas and offering guests the opportunity to more easily and frequently engage one another.
- The use of common spaces is not only aimed at creating improved comfort and connection, but redesigns make

for more open and intuitive environments for guests, offering more choices for how to relax, be entertained, and get work done.

- In-residence bartenders, creating a variety of interactions that increase the level of engagement and offer learning and exploration to guests.
- The continuous redesign of guest rooms to reflect changing habits and offering more thoughtful attention to detail guided by customer input.

Though these examples appear to be outcomes of Marriott's creative response to customer needs and wants, they are actually all manifestations of one key innovation that gave life to all of them. Perhaps the singular most ingenious aspect of the set of the company's innovative offerings is the online and on-site experiences that invite customers to co-create their experience—a set of attractively interactive ways through which customers submit their own ideas and become partners in the design and creation of the company's product offerings and customer experiences. Customers are summoned to participate in creating what Marriott calls "Progress," a way in which visitors to the company's website are encouraged to take part in the design thinking process, and take part in moving from "Idea, to Prototype, to Product." In other words, customers are actively engaging in the design of the products and services *they themselves want to buy.* This *"tell us what you want"* strategy offers a new take on better listening and responding to the consumer. Often, as the aforementioned instances of Marriott's innovations show, it can even happen in real time.

An example of this real-time thinking, and one that exemplifies how the company takes design thinking to a higher level and to its broader audience, is the Marriott hotel in Charlotte, North Carolina. The hotel was conceived to act as a design thinking lab, offering interactive experiences for guests and encouraging them to become participants in the design process. This includes different ways of asking and listening to guest feedback and ideas, and inviting them to provide real-time input through strategically placed customer reaction buttons. Much of the feedback is immediately fed to digital displays throughout the hotel and through which guests can see their participation and influence.

The design eloquence of this innovation is that it contributes to two interdependent and aligned outcomes. Not only is customer engagement and loyalty affected in a positive way, but it has the added benefit of aligning the customer experience to the culture of the company, a culture wherein everyone is engaged in the design and delivery of the customer experience and wherein the use of design thinking is attaining status as a core competency that motivates creativity and performance.

How did it happen? After all, taking the view and realizing design thinking as a key competency doesn't materialize overnight. Rather, it takes some time for it to begin to find its way through an organization, especially one of the size and global breadth of Marriott.

MULTIPLYING ENGAGEMENT

Recognizing the forces of human motivation and energy at play, we decided it was likely best to define it more concisely, leading us to the momentum of the emotional energy that manifests itself in our creativity and innovation as the pull factor. As Kevin Lee, the leader in the design thinking at Visa, so aptly described the pull factor's impact, "Once they experience design thinking, people get evangelized and converted. They become believers in design thinking and its delivery of an experience. They want to get involved." This is consistent across companies that use design thinking and the experience of how it influences cultures. It's in the pull, not the push.

One of the key shifts influenced by an organization's pull factor is the change in how and why decisions about the allocation and use of money and resources are made. Choices and conclusions are now much less a matter of change management and strategies coming from the top of the organization, and more the result of the response to design thinking and the pull created by groups and teams in different parts of the organization. There is a sense of empowerment that engages groups, often comprised of members from across multiple

THE PULL FACTOR PHENOMENON OCCURS IN ALL EMPLOYEE GENERATIONS:

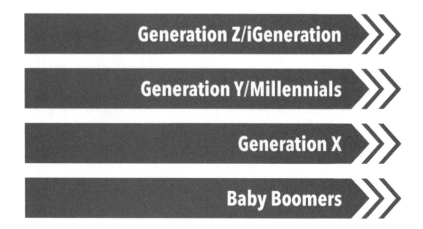

Generation Z/iGeneration

Generation Y/Millennials

Generation X

Baby Boomers

functions and teams, that are focused on confronting and tackling the most pressing problems and the need for new ideas and change.

What we discovered from our research is that the manner in which design thinking is used, and the pull factor it generates, causes leaders—from CEOs to other leaders throughout organizations—to think differently about how to bring it to the forefront of the options and strategies used to solve problems and innovate. Furthermore, it stands to reason that responding to and leveraging the pull factor requires leaders to think differently about how design thinking generates and supports the cultural shifts required to be more innovative. In some cases, it asks leaders to explore what would happen if they turned their accepted change models on their heads, taking an upside-down view of change and innovation in their organizations and how they use money and resources.

In every effort to solve a problem or create a change, there is a tipping point. In older paradigms of change management, the tipping point is reached through the efforts of leaders to chart a course and implement a strategy. From many long-standing and outdated views, the attainment of success requires leaders to identify and engage change champions that assume the role of select campaigners and advocates for the planned change. They act as role models, encouraging others to participate and engage in creating the change. Often, and in most cases it goes unsaid, it is a paradigm that supports the proposition that those not in support of the change will sooner or later comply, be asked to leave, or exit on their own accord.

A PARADIGM SHIFT

Our research informs us to look at it differently and shift our thinking to a new paradigm in which, given the right opportunity and empowerment, people naturally endeavor to solve problems and create change. By pulling and not pushing from the top, the tipping point is much less difficult and, in most cases, less time-consuming to reach. It is leveraged through engagement in different parts and groups within an organization. Furthermore, given the slightest level of empowerment and encouragement, people will engage in the collaboration that is an expression of our collective imagination and the natural consequence of our shared human desire to participate and create together. Although we've often experienced leaders talking in these terms, we've seldom experienced organizations actually doing it—that is, until now. What we find is that, in design thinking cultures, people naturally generate the pull factor required to respond to solving the problem.

At Visa, one of the key contributors to the company's innovative success is this expression of the natural desire to participate and have an impact. It is a coming together of the collective imagination that manifests itself through collaboration. This expressed value for collaboration assures that everyone is thinking beyond each individual's output—beyond themselves and their individual forms of problem-solving and performance. Not only is the goal of alignment a focus, but each person has a charter of responsibility to assure that the partner or partners they are collaborating with always attain success. This "multiplying engagement" model assures that everyone is involved in vetting and contributing to one another's ideas, and leverages the pull factor across functions. Not only does this reinforce internal mechanisms to assure people are invited to participate, it creates myriad outcomes that extend beyond silo-oriented performance indicators and the trappings of unintentional internal competition that people can easily fall prey to. Depending on the scope of problem or design, people will decide how much and for how long to participate. These are all indicators of the pull factor at work.

RETHINKING INVESTMENT IN INNOVATION

For those of you who want to skip ahead and go directly to the "how to" solutions section, we suggest you go directly to finding them in the other chapters of this book and the host of step-by-step guides to design thinking. There you'll find the blueprints, the strategies, and a number of proven how-to approaches to using design thinking. However, if you do decide to take that step, you'll very likely find your way back to this portion of the book. After all, when it comes to best practices, one inevitably comes to the need and responsibility of making good choices as to how to invest—how to wisely and effectively use resources and money—in the successful creation and development of a design thinking culture.

To take a closer look at what this looks like, let's delve back into the Marriott International story. Earlier in this chapter, we shared with you a number of the innovations that the company has delivered to their customers, many of which customers are directly involved in creating.

It began in 2013, when the company's board, CEO Arne Sorenson, and his leadership team identified innovation as the greatest risk to the company's future. In response to this need, they determined that design thinking offered one of the best solutions. Along with this leadership support and an increased focus on innovation as a key competency, the company began by moving from being "the world's #1 hotel company" to becoming "the world's #1 hospitality company," a small shift in strategy that is aligned to its compelling quest to be the leading innovator in its industry.

With the endorsement of Sorenson and the company's board, design thinking was first applied to the company's branding efforts.

Not only was this endeavor a great success, it also drew attention from leadership, and people throughout the organization, to the way in which design thinking offered a new and highly creative and more collaborative means to solve a critical set of problems. Based on the success of its use, design thinking rapidly began to take hold as what would soon become an enterprise-wide approach to more creative and collaborative problem-solving and innovation. This resulted in the understanding that design thinking offered a multiplying effect of innovation, an effect that began in the application of design thinking to one problem (branding) and led to the level of success that it soon began getting noticed by others throughout the company. The result was that it was soon generating a pull factor that began percolating in a variety of groups. Eventually, design thinking began emerging as a powerful force for problem-solving and innovative thinking throughout the company and its culture.

The multiplying effect of innovation resulting from the pull factor is powerful in a number of ways. Eventually, its force is undeniable, influencing how people work without the requirement of a lot of push and direction from the top, and need for detailed strategy from the higher levels of an organization. When this happens, it also becomes less of a game wherein people seek permission or need the authority to use resources from the top of a company. The application of design thinking creates patterns and behaviors that create a more natural means through which people rely less on permission and more on taking their own initiative. As you can imagine, this has a great deal of influence on how people think about how money and resources are used, at all levels of an organization. Just think about the savings involved in not spending needless energy on the politics and planning processes associated with the more traditional forms of problem-solving, and over-directed and constraining methods.

There are also the harder-to-measure expenses that come with the variety of drawbacks resulting from the lack of collaboration that the pull factor impacts in positive ways. Among those affected are the lack of communication, cooperation, turf protection, silos, and the host of dysfunctional behaviors that are typical. And, let's not forget about redundancy and the missed opportunities almost always apparent in most organizations. These are all hidden costs that affect not just the rate of innovation and creativity organizations endure, they become part of the cultural landscape that keep collaboration at bay. Design thinking helps provide a path for moving through these obstacles, resulting in much more efficiency and lowered costs associated with what we most commonly associate with more rigid processes and methods.

These insights and learning were not overlooked at Marriott, a company that prides itself on prudent and self-described conservative financial management. In fact, Marriott offers an example of how the pull factor can, with speed and agility, influence an organization's culture, offering evidence of the pull factor and how it can, in short period of time, have a profound and positive affect—outcomes that extend beyond the outcomes we shared with you and expand far beyond the numerous innovations impacting the customer experience.

Along the way, as a result of design thinking being pulled into various parts of the organization, Marriott has also established itself as one of the planet's best and most progressive employers. The company has received accolades and awards for its devotion to the healthy lifestyles of its employees, its management of a globally diverse workforce, its role in the advancement and advocacy of women's leadership, and its impressive array of programs aimed at creating social benefit. The company was even recognized for the creativity of its outstanding law department. When it comes to an alignment, there's a lot to be said for treating and engaging employees in the same manner as your customers. At Marriott, when it comes to innovation and creating market leadership, there's something special that comes from this thinking.

GETTING *MUCH* MORE FOR LESS

When investing in innovation, we've concluded, based on our research, that innovative companies have traits and beliefs about employee development and engagement in common and that are key contributors to their success.

For starters, the companies in our study are all arriving at the belief that, despite the availability and application of methodical and predictable data-driven and scientific approaches, in the end the core of innovation lies in the human experience. The companies and their leaders all eventually discover (or reach a point of rediscovery) that at the heart of creativity and meaningful innovation are human experience and emotion—hence, the popular application and use of the term *human-centered design.*

In the past, the key factors and deliberate priorities of change strategies and problem-solving, which demonstrate an organization's commitment to innovation, typically orbited around two key resources: time and money. This is particularly true as it relates to the implementation of strategies and methods designed to ensure constant forms of measurement are used and ROIs (return on investment) can be justified. The result is a reliance on data-driven and scientific approaches. The use of methods that limit the exchange of information and ideas holds at bay the human experience and hinders emotional involvement. Such approaches result in developing the use of tools and systems as core competencies that can result in innovation.

The organizations in our research see things differently. As we've shared in other parts of this book, they look at design thinking as a means to focus on and develop *innovation as a core competency,* committing time and dollars, and thereby showing the willingness to invest in its development and application. They also share the view that the interpersonal skills associated with design thinking and innovation are not only warranted, but essential to success.

While the attributes of innovation as a competency are generally seen as a set of softer teamwork skills, they are also recognized as the most challenging for organizations and their employees to manifest and develop. These include the need for open dialogue, sharing ideas, challenging and being challenged, and allowing bigger ideas to emerge. As we mentioned earlier in this chapter, these are skills that are typically not taught or focused on in the traditional—and still widely accepted—approaches to business and executive education. As a result, to overcome this shortcoming and lack of essential interpersonal skills, it becomes a strategic focus to train design thinking facilitators and practitioners. It makes the need for executive training in design thinking practices that much more necessary, including how to effectively role model and reinforce the required communication skills.

The truth about innovative organizations is that their ability to create cutting-edge products and services is a direct reflection of their ability to co-create and innovate internally. Furthermore, without an investment in the development of an innovative workforce and membership, one can hardly expect to have an innovative culture that consistently delivers cutting-edge, emotionally fulfilling customer experiences.

LEARNING TO BE BETTER

Wells Fargo started their foray into design thinking 13 years ago by establishing a user-centered design software development process on the consumer side of their business. It was then transferred over to the business-to-business side as a leaping-off point to expand design thinking for solving problems through multifunctional alignment, prototyping, and consumer feedback. Like many of the 20-plus design thinking–oriented companies we've looked closely into, Wells Fargo used an outside firm to help accelerate understanding and interest in design thinking and as a catalyst to bring new thinking inside the organization. The typical way to engage is to define a manageable project—in this case, using ethnography and prototyping to explore new retail experiences, and look, listen, prototype, test, involve users, and also involve executives.

The power of design thinking can't be denied when people experience it firsthand. Wells Fargo calls their design thinking work Experience Strategy, as they set out to explore new customer experiences. Robin Beers, PhD, is senior vice president, head of design and research at Wells Fargo, and is instrumental in developing their design thinking initiatives. According to Robin, "Design thinking enables a culture of care." She argues that people don't learn as well with statistics, or big data, or spreadsheets, but rather by being engaged, in a more primal manner. She notes:

In the industrial era, the focus was on efficiency. So we break problems down into small parts, and use, for example, Agile or other current efficiency methods to fix the new or broken parts. But design thinking is about holism, and asking what's the big problem? And, how do we achieve alignment to solve this problem? And even more out of the norm, how do we use visual sense making to understand the problem, in order to begin working on solving it?

In other words, she is proposing a quite radical management approach to innovation, but actually one that's quite natural to many people. Robin calls this "conscious collaboration" and recognizes how it brings deep enjoyment and satisfaction. "Using design thinking creates an emotional pull in people. It pulls people in, because people want to be connected, to utilize one another's competencies, and to be involved."

In the end, design thinking is about simplicity and clarity. She says, "Simplicity has to trump everything for the customer." In her group's design thinking workshops, the agenda is straightforward: Your only job today is to think *How might we* _____ *and deliver the best experience for the customer?*

They tell people to "act like a designer today," and the learning curve can be very short. This leads to reframing the problem, collaborating with the customer, conceptual prototyping, and refining. In design thinking sessions with customers, Wells Fargo has saved some large customers "millions" in time savings per day.

Robin also points out that design thinking is very primal; it enables the ability for people to think together, and really think, rather than just running from meeting to meeting. Design thinking, she says, "is non-hierarchal, meaning it's not about your expertise." It's about realizing you don't have to have the answer and being okay with that. For example, design thinking sessions include techniques to level the playing field, so to speak, to make every opinion be heard, such as never letting the most senior person in the room speak first. In this culture, people lean into design thinking once they realize it can be an inherently joyful experience. This actually pulls people into engagement. What's most interesting is that most people want to be pulled in. They just don't often have the opportunities.

This kind of engagement requires expert facilitation, so Wells Fargo has developed a network of trained design thinking facilitators. They are scaling this up significantly to meet internal demand. One might ask: Where does this demand come from? It's the pull factor. It comes from executives who are learning about design thinking and asking how they can get some. It comes from Gen X, Y, and Z employees who want to engage. It comes from senior employees who want to be a part of what's new, not what's old. It comes from customers who want new solutions to old problems. And it comes from within. For within our hearts and minds is the human motivation for inclusion, imagination, and free expression. It is enabled by a culture with a learning mindset, like Wells Fargo.

A NOTE ABOUT WELLS FARGO

Wells Fargo is the world's second-largest bank by market capitalization, and the third-largest bank in the United States by assets. In 2017, Wells Fargo ranked fifth on the *Forbes Magazine* Global 2000 list of largest public companies in the world, and in 2016 ranked 27th on the Fortune 500 list of largest companies in the United States. In 2015, the company was ranked the 22nd-most-admired company in the world, and the seventh most-respected company in the world.

This all changed with their recent sales scandal, resulting in the termination of several executives. Corporate reputations are difficult to build, yet so easy to tarnish. It is our opinion that if Wells Fargo had used design thinking to pull together people to figure out how to increase their number of customers, rather than the push approach that led to fraudulent methods, the results would have been so much better. And the company's reputation, and that of its leadership, may not have been called into question.

8

The Right Problems

"Successful problem solving requires finding the right solution to the right problem. We fail more often because we solve the wrong problem than because we get the wrong solution to the right problem."
—Russell L. Ackoff

One of the earliest and most revealing cases we've heard about the power of design thinking comes from Marco Steinberg, a former professor of architecture at Harvard and director of the Helsinki Design Lab in Finland. Marco shared this story with Tom when they participated in a creative workshop at the Lab in Helsinki. According to Marco, sometime in the late 1940s the city of Helsinki had a very nice public swimming pool. After World War II, it enjoyed a robust membership and had a lovely synchronized swimming program. Over a short period of time, the pool membership began declining, so much so that the budget to maintain the pool was significantly reduced. With lower usage and lower budget for maintenance, things began to spiral down, and eventually the pool fell in disarray.

The Helsinki City Council was pretty discouraged about this. In the early 1950s, they decided they needed to build a new swimming pool and gathered significant funds to do so. They hired a leading architect to design a great new public swimming pool for the city.

The City Council members were all quite excited the day the architect came to present the design of the new pool. They were quite surprised and initially disappointed when they saw that the only thing the architect brought to the meeting was a public bus schedule. In diligently doing his research about why people stopped using the pool, he discovered that the city had terminated the bus line that made a stop by the swimming pool after normal working hours. To accommodate people traveling to and from work, the bus route that went by the pool only ran from about 7 a.m. to 6 p.m. But swimmers used the pool complex before or after work, not during working hours. The architect told the City Council members something along the lines of "The reason people don't come to your pool anymore is not because you've got a bad pool design. It's because they can't get there before or after work when they have free time."

> "My therapist set half a glass of water in front of me and asked if I was a pessimist or an optimist. So, I drank the water and told him I was a problem solver."
>
> —Unknown

PROBLEM FINDING

In simple terms, in design thinking a key to success is in first finding the right problem. Delivering a good solution requires one to first focus on finding out what is most important to creating the best solution for the customer. For this reason, great design thinking always begins with a focus on the customer and understanding the human experience. This includes getting as much information and finding out as much as possible about what is motivating the customer, as well as the contextual aspects of the situation. It's important to take a broader view and explore and discover what one can about the environment and conditions the customer is a part of. The same holds true for solving internal problems, those that affect processes and systems, thereby ultimately impacting the members of the organization.

When people in an organization develop the competency and knack for finding the right problem, they identify and confront issues in a timely manner. This not only helps to avoid unnecessary conflict that results from unattended and resolved problems, the tendency is the organization performs at a higher level. There is improvement in time to market, quality of product and service, quality of design, customer experience—you get the picture.

As we all know, when it comes to solving problems, the best results come about from digging as deeply as possible into the problem to find the root cause. As Marco Steinberg's Helsinki pool story illustrates, unless we make an effort to explore and engage the wider spectrum of people and possibilities, and think more systemically and with greater curiosity, organizations can spend a lot of time and money chasing the wrong solution.

One of the ways to finding the "true what" is by un-isolating the problem. It's fairly natural for people to want to find the quickest and most readily available solution. This means looking at what's right in front of us and then most likely finding the quickest fix. Sometimes this also ends up adding complexity rather than finding the simplest solution. Effectively finding the true "what" requires being able to explore the scope of contextual possibilities and uncovering whether a problem is internal, external, process-related, or systems-related. By doing so, one can better understand the context and find the real problem.

The ability to find the right problem is an attribute that allows the organizations in our study group to consistently perform at the level they do. It certainly doesn't happen every time. If a solution is found, is implemented, and doesn't get the desired result, the need to keep exploring is not abandoned. Rather, design thinking organizations look at it as another challenge, another step on the path to greatness and the never-ending pursuit of their purpose and desired outcomes. On the other end of the spectrum, regardless of how good an outcome they generate, they display the organizational intelligence of curiosity and are on the constant lookout and exploration as to what else is possible: what's next.

A good way to approach finding the right problem to solve is the development of a framework within the organization that represents the accepted approach of its members. From SAP comes a good example of such a framework, a solution they designed to respond to the need to focus efforts on better applying their well-developed design thinking capability.

At SAP, the definition of innovation is *problem finding* × *problem-solving.*

In the previous chapter, we provided insight into the scaling of design thinking at SAP. Because the company has such a long history with design and design thinking, SAP keeps the use of it focused by stressing that innovation and customer empathy are ways of problem-solving, and keeping the focus on solving the right problem. And though some would call it creative problem-solving, it's really more about finding the right problems to solve. To that effect and to create greater clarity, the SAP mindset is to focus design thinking methodology on "problem finding," and viewing design thinking as the means through which to have the ability to scale creativity. They accomplish this by using the formula of "problem finding × problem-solving."

SAP has a high degree of ownership in how they promote and manage their innovative culture. The culture is represented by two key descriptive elements: "Driven by Innovation" and "Innovation in Action." In everything they do, the company is dedicated to applying design thinking to achieve innovation. This includes research, development, partnering, and their relationship to the customer.

The action orientation toward innovation reflects its measure that design is not a noun, but rather a verb—a call to action: "SAP innovations across our products, technologies, and programs are motivated by a desire to improve people's lives, at scale. We use our unsurpassed global reach, our relevance, and our relationships to drive positive change for individuals, organizations, and societies."[1] This is a tall order and deeply emotional pursuit, and results in the reinforcement of digging deeper to find the right problems that need to be solved. The scaling of design thinking at SAP is not just about how many people in the organization are trained and applying design thinking. SAP's vision calls for a much broader application and mindset for its application to innovation at a global scale, to explore and solve the greater problems of our world.

WICKED PROBLEMS

In the world of design thinking, thanks to some great public relations, the design company IDEO helped popularize the term *wicked problems*. The origin of the idea of wicked problems and coining of the term is credited to the German-born design theorist Horst Rittel, who is seen as a pioneer of design who looked at planning, engineering, and policy-making as forms of design. He applied the term to the problems of social policy, which he thought, in light of the multitude of competing human interests, were rather impossible to solve.[2] His were some of the first forays in the use of design thinking into what is categorized as systems design, the Fourth Order of design.

In the early 1970s, while working at the University of California at Berkeley, Rittel partnered with fellow UC of Berkeley professor Melvin Webber to challenge the construct of how social problems were solved. Together they established a set of criteria for wicked problems, among them that: the solution depends on how a problem is framed; stakeholders have differing views and mindsets for understanding a problem; the solution is only as good as the resources available to solve it and can therefore change over time; and because conditions change and the problem is seen as dynamic, the solution is never really definitive and can always be improved upon. Wicked problems are those that, in light of their enormity or difficulty, most often go unaddressed and unresolved.[3]

"In the statement of the problem lies the solution."
—Charles Eames

One of the key aspects of design thinking is taking the approach to a problem, whether it is considered wicked or not, as human-centered. It cannot be solved through just scientific approaches. It brings back into light and focuses on the significance of human motivation and emotion. In relationship to the context of organizations and their cultures, wicked problems are often the difficult ones because they cross functions and systems, and therefore would have multiple "owners," who often have different agendas or views of success. They can be the source of the greatest ideas and innovations.

In our research, we found that a key to the success of design thinking cultures is an ability to identify and pursue the most significant challenges, regardless of the perceived owner. They demonstrate the ability to cross boundaries and functions to identify and solve the right problems, not just the superficial or incremental problems, or making a new widget. A common trait of design thinking cultures is their aim to identify and solve the root causes of problems. They are not tempted by the short-term success of low-hanging fruit. The organizations in our study group are not driven to just creating new ideas. Rather, they have a need for better ideas and finding the right innovation. Design thinking cultures are not about just brainstorming or ideation, they are about developing a competency to identify and then focus on what is important, and to solve that. They keep coming back to the principles of human-centered design and service design.

GHOST TOWN TURNAROUND

A great example of finding the right problem is Kaiser Permanente's seminal work several years ago creating solutions to close the hole in patient care created by shift changes in its hospital nursing staffs. At first glance, it would make sense that the nurses could solve the problem by immediately paying attention to patients as soon as they came on shift. Yet, when they did, they still found themselves being pulled away to communicate with the nurses ending their shifts or to find patient information.

Using design thinking, the first step was to engage all the stakeholders, including nurses, patients, and the array of hospital staff. The discovery process led to the understanding that the problem that needed to be solved was how nurses exchanged patient information between shifts—a process that typically took 45 minutes or more and delayed the arriving nurses' first contact with their patients. Not surprisingly, the project revealed that patients felt a "hole in their care" during shift changes. In fact, many patients described hospitals as a "ghost town" during shift changes. Worse, nurses compiled and exchanged patient information in idiosyncratic and unreliable ways (some even scrawled notes on their scrubs). Important details were often left out or care that had already been provided was needlessly repeated.[4]

What came to be called Nurse Knowledge Exchange (NKE) created a process for passing on higher-quality information more quickly and reliably. Now the exchange occurs at the patient's bedside rather than at the nurses' station. Patients are encouraged to participate, making it less likely that anything important relating to their care will fall through the cracks. New software helps nurses compile information in a standard format throughout their shifts. And they are less likely hours later to experience a jolt of panic that they've forgotten to communicate something important. Nurse Knowledge Exchange has since been rolled out to all Kaiser Permanente hospitals.

According to Christi Zuber, a member of the Innovation Consultancy team, the most significant result of the group's work is bringing human-centered design to the organization. This provided a tangible, teachable approach to innovation, a language, and an infrastructure to support it before that was common or understood within any industry, and within healthcare in particular. When asked what she thinks is the Consultancy's greatest accomplishment, Christi told us, "I have always loved our Nurse Knowledge Exchange work. It effects the way nearly 8,000 nurses engage with patients every 24 hours, seven days a week, 365 days a year. And that's in our hospitals alone. It's an approach that's touted by IHI [Institute for Healthcare Improvement] and has spread around the globe."

KAISER PERMANENTE

Founded in 1945, Kaiser Permanente is the largest not-for-profit integrated healthcare delivery system in the United States, providing high-quality, coordinated, and affordable care. Headquartered in Oakland, California, Kaiser has 38 hospitals, and more than 200,000 employees across seven geographic regions, serving more than 10.6

million members. In 2016, it reached $64.6 billion in annual operating revenue.

Design thinking is embedded in Kaiser's culture and enjoys a prominent place in the organization with significant influence on how the organization operates. The vehicle through which Kaiser integrates design thinking across the span of the organization is the Innovation Consultancy, an internal innovation and design team "working to bring joy and simplicity to the care experience."

Established in 2003, the Innovation Consultancy started as a first-of-its-kind experiment to explore the value of human-centered design in healthcare. It is self-described as "a unique team that brings fresh methods that liberate patients, frontline providers and managers to discover, design and implement new ways to improve the care experience of our patients and the work experience of our caregivers." During the past 10 years, Kaiser has trained about 15,000 people in some form of design thinking.

REFRAMING THE PROBLEM

Another early and foundational case study in using design thinking to solve the right problem—not just the problem they thought they had—is P&G's development of the Swiffer. Preceding this innovation, P&G CEO A.G. Lafley made a declaration: He wanted P&G to become the best consumer products company in the world at design. They were already perhaps the best at brand building, but he felt it wasn't enough. He established the position of VP of design, and put in place Claudia Kotchka, an accountant, to run it. Fortunately, Claudia is a savvy business leader, and she began to surround herself with some of the best design management and design thinking people out there. Under her leadership P&G hired some 350 design managers to run their design and innovation initiatives more professionally, within the company and with the user in mind, and let go many of their external marketing, brand, and communication agencies.

The Swiffer come about strictly as a result of finding the right problem. P&G wanted to build business in the mop category. According to Continuum, a product design and innovation firm, they were hired to create a better mop, and part of the project brief included the following information: On average, in the United States, the kitchen floor is cleaned about once a week for up to 45 minutes, the kitchen floor is swept daily, and counter tops are cleaned twice a day. Mops are typically used, in fact, with the following applications: sponge mop 42 percent, string mop 26 percent, and cloth mop 17 percent of the time. What's more, 30 percent of households buy 1.5 mops or brooms each year. That said, in the retailing of mops there is no brand recognition. It was not big business as it is now. At that time, mops and brooms were a $300 million/year sales category, but P&G wanted more revenue. This statistical marketing information did little to inform the design team how to design a better mop. What more would a design thinker need to know? Well, it turns out that there's a lot more to know.

A small team, an industrial designer, ethnographic researcher, and others set out to explore how, when, and why people mop their kitchen floors. Here's what they found: People clean the floor, and then they clean the thing that they use to clean the floor. This involves water, actually making mud. Cleaning implements, like mops, clean through entrainment of dirt. But the better the thing is at cleaning the floor, the more difficult it is to clean.

The small design research team began to ask questions, such as: Why do you need to use water to pick up dirt? Why make mud? How much water is used and wasted in the process? And how much time do people spend cleaning the mop of mud, versus mopping? They asked P&G: Isn't there anything that can pick up dirt other than water? So P&G came up with a chemical and the designers put it on a disposable pad, and the Swiffer was born. *Marvelous*, the product managers at P&G thought. *We'll sell the holder, and tons of disposable cleaning pads, instead of a reusable mop. Just like razor blades.*

Since that design thinking success, the Swiffer has made P&G billions, and in so doing helped users by solving the real problem: cleaning the floor, versus making mud. Today, P&G has revenue in excess of $65 billion and has the largest lineup of leading brands in its industry, with 22 brands with more than $1 billion in annual sales, and another 19 brands generating approximately $500 million or more in annual sales. Swiffer continues to be a fast-growing line of cleaning products and tools, including the Swiffer, WetJet, Duster, Vac, and Dust and Shine.

More than a decade has passed since the success of the Swiffer project, and P&G continues to leverage design thinking internally. Evidence shows that design thinking coupled with sustained intervention helps the company achieve big business building ideas. Design thinking at P&G has come a long way in its development and, despite its fair share of ups and downs, continues to thrive in the culture. The long-term success at P&G demonstrates how design thinking is helping the company creatively confront and solve the right problems, some which challenge the wicked end of the problem spectrum.

THE INFLUENCE OF EMPATHY

At the outset, an emphasis on empathizing with the customer is essential. Empathy allows us to understand and share the same feelings that others feel, and through which we explore what it's like to put ourselves in other people's shoes and connect with how they might be feeling about their problem, circumstance, or situation. Without empathy, the idea and potential of human-centered design isn't fulfilled.

We also found that these organizations are not just great at creating new products and services, but also solving internal problems. It takes a special attitude to embellish empathy for working peers, but when you do all manner of process problems, problems that cross touch points, silo challenges, and user experience problems become a snap. These innovations result in the capability to design the solutions to larger, more complex problems, including the application of design thinking to its powerful use in the not-for-profit and public sectors.

It is also why design thinking is ideal in solving problems that reach across organizations and their various functions, as well as optimizing the design of products and services. This becomes powerful in solving problems like the undertaking of P&G's re-imagining of its employee proposition. Defining the problem well requires getting clear on the needs and insights of its employees, an endeavor to integrate individual and group agendas with that of the company. Whether internal or external, the showing of empathy and listening to convey the desire for understanding is essential.

Getting the best result requires paying attention to and empathizing with employees at different levels, as well as leadership from across and at the different levels of the organization, with multiple owners. No doubt, this will ultimately challenge the ability of any organization to go to deeper levels of understanding and be open to the learning experiences it will create. And, those participating will need to be attuned to the shared understanding of what the problems are and the shared opportunity to resolving them. In a complex system of multiple points of interest and experience, design thinking offers the best opportunity for results to what we would consider a wicked problem.

Among the takeaways from the examples in this chapter, we'd like to emphasize three key points. The first is the articulation of consumer insights, the development of a deep understanding of the consumer experience, and the unearthing of unarticulated user needs. In the case of Kaiser Permanente's NKE, the understanding of the nurses' experience further helped to define the core problem that needed to be solved. Design thinking, by engaging and empathizing with all stakeholders involved, provides a means through which to understand the point of view and needs of everyone involved.

This leads us to the second key point: the power and role of design thinking in the identification of the right problem that needed to be solved.

Lastly, it is important to realize that each of the examples reflects the unique nature of the culture of each organization. P&G, SAP, and Kaiser Permanente have their own unique cultures, yet all successfully apply—and have successfully scaled—design thinking throughout their organizations. From this observation, we can draw two important conclusions:

1. Without sacrificing any of its core principles and elements, or lessen its capability to achieve the desired outcome,

design thinking can be tailored to align to the unique culture of any organization.

2. Once the capability of design thinking is experienced, the pull factor seems to be unavoidable. This leads to greater innovation and a continued promise of greater levels of problem-solving, innovation, and performance.

9

Culture Awareness

"When you show deep empathy toward others, their defensive energy goes down, and positive energy replaces it. That's when you get more creative in solving problems."
—Stephen Covey

Like a lot of processes and systems that are introduced or strategically implemented into an organization, many either fail to be integrated or lose traction over time. There are a host of reasons this happens, including the lack of support from an organization's members and leaders. These are indicators of a far more powerful aspect of implementation: culture.

Design thinking, like other ideas and strategic solutions, if introduced and implemented without considering how it will fit an organization's culture, can fail. In the majority of cases this is not the result of the strategies or processes being bad ideas. Rather, they fail to stick because they do not fit the culture of the organization or are not implemented in a manner that aligns to how the organization creates success. This can easily lead us back to the question of why it always has to be about culture. Because it is!

Organizations are forms of complex social systems that are shaped and formed by human interaction. Therefore, it becomes important to understand how an organization's culture can respond to and support the variety of human needs that manifest themselves in behaviors and interactions. The culture keys we provided in Chapter 4, including roles, how decisions are made, problem-solving processes, and definitions of teamwork, are some of the means through which we can influence a culture that responds to people's various emotional needs. The better an organization is able to respond to human emotion, the more aligned it is. Furthermore, the more aligned the use of design thinking is to the culture, the greater the likelihood for success.

Through our research, we found that leaders in design thinking organizations tend to be more knowledgeable about their cultures, and how to successfully implement the strategies and methods of design thinking. If we take the first half of our definition of culture and focus on the aspect of individual and collective success, we realize that design thinking naturally shifts the definition of success to include a focus on higher levels of collaboration and engagement from their members. The shifts in how people engage in problem-solving result in changes in how challenges are addressed, how decisions are made, how people are rewarded, and how their contributions are celebrated by not just leaders, rather by one another. We also find that people work with one another with greater levels of empathy.

ORGANIZATIONAL EMPATHY

Empathy is at the heart of design, and is the core of innovation and creativity. In light of its importance in design thinking and because of the increased use of the term in organizations, we thought it worthwhile to visit its definition. And, because both empathy and sympathy relate to emotion, and are often mistakenly applied or wrongly used interchangeably, it's important to differentiate one from the other.

Empathy is putting yourself in someone else's shoes and understanding how they feel, thereby having the ability to relate to and experience the emotion of another person. Sympathy is caring and understanding for the suffering or condition of others and feeling compassion, sorrow, or pity for the hardships that another person encounters. A person doesn't need to have sympathy for another person to understand how that other person feels.

Based on this meaning of empathy, organizational empathy is defined as an attribute of culture demonstrated by the ability of its people to relate to and experience the emotion of others. This definition and its application have a great deal to do with how aware leaders are about the motivations of people within the organization, and how they approach the use of design thinking. In other words, it's important to be able to understand the ability of an organization's membership to engage one another with empathy. It is also essential to understand the motivation that underlies how they engage in it.

Organizational empathy is also a key to overcoming the typical barriers to collaboration and cooperative teamwork between groups, functions, or teams. Through the use of empathy in design thinking, people are able to collaborate and cooperate with one another across the typical boundaries that exist between functions and groups, as well as experience one another more intentionally when in the service to each other as internal customers. This can scale across an organization and goes well beyond the focus on having empathy for customers. It is further reinforced by leaders who, when at their best, also demonstrate empathy for their employees. This role-modeling and reinforcement of empathy are key to the model of seek first to understand, then begin to solve. Because design thinking naturally shifts the definition of success to one that includes a focus on higher levels

Organizational Empathy:
An attribute of an organization's culture demonstrated by the ability of its people to relate to and experience the emotion of others.

of collaboration and engagement from its members, it emphasizes the need for aligned leadership.

The story about Kaiser Permanente's creation of the Nurse Knowledge Exchange (NKE) in Chapter 8 is a good example of shifting the definition of success from merely providing an isolated solution to shortening the time that patients are left without care, to one that also responds to the internal challenges faced by the nurses and related staff. The broader involvement not only demonstrates a willingness to empathize and understand the internal issues that confront employees, the desire to understand their emotional response invited them to participate and feel more engaged.

In a healthcare culture typically perceived as more hierarchal with clear role definitions, this creates a shift the mindset of who is involved in solving problems and how decisions are made. Such shifts in mindset are further reinforced and embedded in a culture through the likelihood of the success associated with a new way of doing things. In the case of Kaiser, the global recognition its NKE program received helped to increase the value of the broader participation and sense of empowerment that design thinking brought to the culture.

The kind of success that Kaiser and the story of Intuit and its training of all of its employees point out, is that having an awareness of a culture allows leaders to interpret what will and will not work in their organizations, and what changes are necessary to creating the shifts that increase the likelihood of success. This relates to the culture keys and how they affect the approach to using design thinking that an organization needs to take. The more aligned the strategy is to the culture, the greater the likelihood of success. As well, the 12 keys provide insight into the changes that may be required to allow for the organization to successfully engage in the use of design thinking. Among others, these can include changes in hiring practices, organizational structure, reward and celebration, teaming, and role definitions. Intuit also includes training and development. These make up a set of important strategic decisions.

Eventually, there are shifts in the origin and use of power and influence. In other words, design thinking is used as a tool for cultural change, directly impacting the level in which their people engage in being more creative and future-oriented thinking. These changes are evidenced through the ways in which people see their influence and contribution to the innovation in products, services, and process improvements; engage in and relate the value of their work; and work to increase their level of performance. Furthermore, through a deeper understanding of culture, leaders and their organizations are better able to leverage their organizational empathy and further humanize innovation.

CULTURAL INTEGRATION

As was the case with many of the organizations in our study group, design thinking was introduced to GE Healthcare in the last decade. Robert Schwartz, the company vice president of design and user experience, started it in 2009. Since that time, they've trained between 5,000 and 6,000 people in design thinking, including 1,200 people in the last year alone. In the makeup of the organization, several people at director levels are running their design thinking training and facilitation programs. This includes everything from two-hour coaching sessions to two-day intensive workshops, and everything in between. The work they do is not limited to the United States. They deliver workshops and support around the globe, including across Europe and in India, China, and Latin America.

In recognition of the home to Thomas Edison's lab in Menlo Park, New Jersey, the name of the design thinking program is appropriately named Menlo. To embrace this cultural history they have even gone so far as to create a new typeface for the identity of this design thinking program, which is patterned after the handwriting of Thomas Edison. This is an example of the design director, along with other leaders, helping employees remember the history and the values of the brand, in particular as they relate to design and innovation. As we experienced with several of the organizations in our study group, the branding of a design thinking program gives employees a sense of increased value to how things get done, helps carry forward cultural values and nuances, and conveys a sense of uniqueness. We see the same approach of linking current design initiatives back to the core roots of the brand at many companies, including P&G, Intuit, and Kaiser Permanente.

The positioning statement for Menlo is "A flexible design thinking framework rooted in simpler times when basic tools and a little imagination can give you powerful solutions." Linking back to the work of Thomas Edison, they say that to improve something, he would try 10,000 ideas in search of a solution. Edison's legacy, dating back 140 years, is in alignment with one of the key components of design thinking: trying a lot of things with the willingness to fail fast. An interesting observation is that, although the design thinking initiative at GE Healthcare has led to many great product and service innovations, they only comprise about 10 percent of their design thinking outcomes. The other 90 percent are related to outcomes involving the solving of business problems and creating new business innovation models.[1]

The design thinking initiatives at GE Healthcare are orchestrated in three primary areas. The first is a focus on design thinking as the means through which to innovate, and includes innovation ideation, human-centered design, customer experience, and service design. The second is focused on simply good design, good design operations, good design organizations, good design strategy, and high-quality design. The third is corporate culture, which includes its brand intention.

When we asked how design thinking influences corporate culture, the response was that employees believe that design thinking is more than an influence on the company's culture. Rather, it is a part of its culture. Of the more than 330,000 employees of GE, 56,000 people are employed in GE Healthcare alone and 5,000 employees are in customer hospitals. Within GE Healthcare, the design thinking department keeps close records of the projects they run, the people they influence, and the results of these projects. This last part of the equation is telling.

GE Healthcare, like the whole of GE, has an expertise culture. By nature, expertise cultures approach problem-solving through analytic-driven processes. Return on investment (ROI) and measurable results are key ingredients in how decisions are made. Expertise cultures also engage in the continuous improvement of processes and systems. To test their ideas and progress toward goals, the speed of delivery, adherence to quality and implementation standards, and performance outcomes that demonstrate progress toward innovation are typically closely watched and measured. The same holds true for design thinking. First, it is tested as a process, and when it generates proven results, it is then expanded through the organization.

GE Healthcare's expertise culture approaches design thinking as a competency, an element of expertise that is required to show its value through its ability to have a direct and measurable effect on return and a demonstrated influence on how well the organization innovates. In an expertise culture, ideas are only good if they are executed to create value.

This differs from a participation culture, in which design thinking is foremost valued and measured as a means through which to increase participation and leverage inclusion as the path to innovation. In an authenticity culture, the foremost value of design thinking that gets paid attention to is how it creates greater levels of openness, and the leveraging of individual and collective creativity. What matters most is how it provides a means through which individuals and the whole of the organization can actualize in pursuit of it idealistic-focused outcomes. Through the lens of each culture, although design thinking provides a very consistent framework and process, it is valued differently.

> The more aligned the use of design thinking is to the culture, the greater the likelihood of success.

DEUTSCHE TELEKOM

Another example of a cultural alignment is the German communication company Deutsche Telekom. It also established its design thinking function with an emphasis on using it as a tool for innovation and collaboration. In its organizational structure, it sits under the senior vice president of design. From there, design thinking is intended to reach all the company's employees and bring about a change in how the organization innovates. Though the story behind how design thinking was implemented is unique to Deutsche Telekom, it is another excellent case study of how a culture that thrives on expertise uses design thinking as a means to increase its competencies. The company's Telekom Design group now leads its efforts.

The arrival of design thinking at Deutsche Telekom also started with a CEO's capability to see design thinking as a key strategic element of the organization. It's also a great example of a culture that now places the development of human capability and competency above overdependence on its technology. Behind it all is the influence of a few experts in design thinking who, by nature of their competency, have the influence to shift the thinking of a large organization to create the impetus for the redesign of an entire company.

It all began when CEO Timotheus Höttges went to a Stanford d.school workshop and fell in love with the power of design thinking. He then decided to go back for another training, this time taking 80 of his top executives with him. From a culture influence viewpoint, that's pretty powerful stuff. The CEO and the entire senior executive team of a company all trained together at d.school's Design Thinking Bootcamp. Together, they found design thinking to be a great way to blend and integrate business process with design process. As a result, and shortly after their Design Thinking Bootcamp experience, they formed the internal program and created an employee training initiative.

One of the key questions that needed to be answered was who would take ownership of the program. This is not an unusual aspect of expertise-type cultures. As the culture most recognizes competency, the question of who will own a function or program, is intended to be answered by figuring out what group will be the most competent in executing it. This dynamic of who owns what is a natural consequence of the culture's effort to maximize the use of specific competencies. It is also considered an important element for success. Therefore, more often than not, the best approach to introducing design thinking into an expertise culture is to organize it as a specific function (like marketing, HR, or operations) and operating in service to the rest of the organization.

The designated function approach provides two culturally aligned outcomes. First, it allows for the measurement of specific outcomes and ROI. Second, it allows for the design thinking owners to establish their expertise and value. This results in people in the organization wanting to utilize the team's expertise and resulting in the increase in the pull factor. Even though leadership mandates the use of design thinking, it still has to pass the competency and value test. Once its value is experienced, the level of interest and engagement in design thinking increases. Eventually the pull factor is increased to the point where the organization comes to the realization that every member ought to be trained in design thinking.

At Deutsche Telekom, after some discussion as to what group would take ownership of the design thinking program, it was decided that the design group and human resources would run it together. Soon, they developed it into a program allowing every employee to log into the company's employee development tool (provided via HR) and engage in design thinking training. The shifts and eventual transformation of the culture can be observed, as can the effect on the culture type itself. As a part of its success, the design thinking group has developed a set of worldwide tools and training that all of its more than 220,000 employees have access to. In 2016 alone, they ran 5,500 design thinking sessions. The success of Deutsche Telekom's program has not gone unnoticed. Airbus, J.A. Henckels, and other European companies are now benchmarking with Deutsche Telecom as they introduce and implement design thinking.

The design thinking program at Deutsche Telekom is focused on some key themes, such as collaborate to innovate, that design thinking is a mindset, that design is a team sport, and that design thinking is too important to be left to designers alone. Design thinking has made its transformation from a buzzword into a business strategy. Based on seven years of experience, the Telekom Design team, through its Design Academy, delivers the methods, principles, and tools of design thinking that are creating a sustainable mind shift across the major parts of the company.

The team also runs a Customer Lab, where customers are invited to participate in every phase of the development process, beginning with understanding customer needs, to getting feedback on ideas and prototypes, and with the refinement of existing solutions. In an inclusive fashion, and in alignment with design thinking values, the team describes itself as a group of unique contributors: "We are designers, creators, thinkers, doers, parents, professionals, workers, managers, experts, colleagues, and friends. We are Telekom Design."

CULTURE SHIFTS

In short, Deutsche Telekom has come to recognize design thinking as a matter of culture and a key to its innovative success. In 2016 alone, the company garnered 142 international design awards from most of the most prestigious design organizations in the world, including the Red Dot Design Award, Clio Awards, and UX Design Awards. CEO Timotheus Höttges was named CEO of the Year at the 2015 World Communication Awards. This kind of success is important, reinforcing the recognition associated with its emphasis on the development of individual competency and how it feeds collective innovation.

The design thinking program integrates well with the organization's culture because the fundamental beliefs in the company are that the customer experience is of the highest value, and that design thinking brings customer input directly into their programs, processes, projects, and products. This link to design thinking as a core competency is an important one, affecting employee behavior and their relationships with their customers. This has a beneficial influence on an expertise culture that has a history of strong power orientation, is hierarchal, and has a hero culture.

The result is that design thinking helps them have more people involved in problem-solving and innovating, and democratizing decision-making so that it even involves customers. The insight is that this integration has been incredibly powerful in helping to manage the corporate culture and more effectively shift it from a hero culture of hierarchy to a more collaborative, customer-centric one. The commitment to a design thinking way of working also helps resolve how disagreements get managed, and the company has found a greater sense of collaboration in solving the real problems.

In the end, people believe that the use of design thinking has influenced the culture in a way that leads to increased corporate creativity. Although design thinking is hard to measure, people feel that it helps in reaching across silos and functions to solve the real problems at hand. They can intuitively feel the influence. As a stated part of their corporate culture, everyone is expected to participate in design thinking training. In exploring the influence of this approach, they found three reasons why people want to take the training:

1. A lot of people are just really excited to learn about design thinking.
2. It's a great way to advance their personal career. In other words, it's an important skill to develop.
3. The boss says so.

There may be some level of peer pressure in an organization that uses design thinking as extensively as Deutsche Telekom. However, as they would argue, that's a good thing.

In the case of Deutsche Telekom, as with the other organizations in our study group, the more leaders are aware of the cultures they lead, the more they are able to align how to implement and integrate design thinking—and the more they are able to understand what influences in the culture will get in the way of their success and what misalignments to avoid. That being said, even in the cases in which leaders were unaware, the cultures they led naturally informed them as to what did and didn't work. This provides us with strong evidence that the level of openness that design thinking provides for will help any organization better understand its culture and have a positive influence on it, even if at first it's a bit messy. We also observed that, given the support of leadership, design thinking will provide people with the means to find the right problem to solve, including those that directly involve the culture—and leadership. The one thing that can ultimately get in the way of success is the resistance of leaders to change.

WHAT ELSE WE FOUND

In exploring our study group and their unique cultures, we found that most have expertise-type cultures. We concluded that this is likely the result of two key factors. First, of the three culture types expertise cultures typically struggle the most with a lack of communication and cooperation, the overcoming of silos, dysfunctional disagreement, and the hierarchy and control that can get in the way of the collaboration and engagement required to attain greater levels of innovation. Design thinking presents a solution that can influence an expertise culture to address and resolve these issues and remove the barriers to collaboration and the resulting innovation.

Second, when we put together the study group, we added organizations that we were pointed to by members of the first several design thinking companies we began our research with. This could very well be an aspect of the intuitive means through which they associate with one another as being similar in the implementation of design thinking, and how they see each other as being successful in the use of design thinking in creating change, shifting cultures, and achieving greater levels of innovation.

We also explored our own data that shows that, of three culture types, the majority of organizations that we have consulted with in our practices are expertise cultures. This can be explained in a number of ways, but most likely is the history of scientific management and its influence on how organizations are structured to leverage competency and expertise. That being said, as every culture is unique, the use of design thinking to deconstruct a culture to explore why it operates the way it does and to explore what's working, and what's not, is a powerful first step.

Lastly, we concluded that regardless of an organization's culture type, the more aligned the strategy and approach in which design thinking is implemented are to the culture of the organization, the greater the likelihood of success. This is especially true if design thinking is used as the means through which to design the implementation. This approach provides a clear signal from leadership in support of its use for producing change, especially as it pertains to culture. Success requires that leaders are aware of and understand the cultures they lead. Lastly, we came to the conclusion that the single most formidable contributor to the failure of design thinking in an organization is the lack of leadership alignment and support.

Curious Confrontation

*"We're in a world now where it's not enough
to be smart. You have to be curious....
That level of intelligence is rare."*
—Barry Diller

Some 40 years ago, in the wake of the Bangladesh famine crisis, the founders of the Hunger Project took on one of humankind's greatest challenges, ending human hunger. It wasn't long before they came to the realization that the usual charity responses and resolutions wouldn't work. They recognized that past efforts did not provide the right solutions because the right problems had not been identified. The key question that needed to be answered was not "How do we do what is being done better?" but "What's missing in the work of ending hunger?"

To broaden and deepen their problem-solving capability, and to think more creatively, they engaged the help of a group of experts and consultants. With the help of the group, they began a deeper inquiry and concluded that it wasn't a matter of throwing money, and more money, at feeding people. At that time, they concluded that the real problem was the lack of political will. In Africa, where women were in the role of farmers, they found poor leadership and a lack of government focus on agriculture. When they confronted this issue further, and followed their curiosity, they realized that the real problem was a matter of gender relationships. Though women had the primary responsibility for the feeding and care of the communities they lived in, they were the least empowered. Each time the organization reinvented itself it required the ability to confront itself, and its stakeholders, to look for what is true.

Confronting the truth and continuously acting from a place of curiosity is not easy. By looking for what was missing, they found the path to strategically reinvent, shifting from the putting of time and energy into education in richer and wealthier countries, to bottom-up development in underdeveloped and impoverished areas of the world. As John Coonrod, the Hunger Project's executive vice president, explains:

> Learning how to reinvent has been part of our process. We had to stop doing what we thought we were good at and start addressing what was missing. Not knowing what was next can be hard sometimes. We had to accept that we didn't know what was next always or how to get there. We referred to it as "climbing a mountain in the fog." We had to shift our resources and get everyone on board.
>
> And then we found out that while leadership was on board, we had failed to engage donors. They didn't understand the change. To do that, we had to educate them and shift their mindset. Instead of calling them "donors," we started calling them "investors." What we learned was that in making strategic shifts, we have to include everyone.

In the 1990s, the Hunger Project once again reinvented itself. To confront gender issues at the local and individual levels, the strategy shifted to focus on the transformation of gender relations. However, this time they started with a focus on the broad engagement of investors and creating internal and external alignment. As John points out:

At the heart, ending hunger is about unleashing the human spirit and human dignity. The key to ending hunger is knowing who hungry people truly are. If given a chance, they will end their own hunger. It is about people being able to be in charge of their own lives and destiny. To not be denied the most basic of human rights and principles so that they can be able and capable of taking action in their own lives. Awareness creation is the starting point of a staged program of building people's confidence, leadership, organizations and skills so that they can set and successfully achieve their own goals. We have a range of capabilities and structures to get things done.

In 1990, in response to typical top-down and charitable responses to hunger, which were often too inefficient and inflexible to meet the challenge of hunger, the Hunger Project, together with the Planning Commission of India, pioneered a new, decentralized, holistic, people-centered approach known as Strategic Planning in Action (SPIA). This methodology turned traditional planning on its head: The Hunger Project would bring all sectors together, identify a critical gap or opportunity for synergy, and then launch catalytic projects, which would reveal new pathways for action. More than 20,000 communities in Asia, Africa, and Latin America have applied SPIA to empower people to achieve lasting improvements in health, education, nutrition, and family income.

The leadership of the Hunger Project shows the ability to confront the truth about the context that they were operating in and, through being curious, inquire and explore what changes they and the organization needed to go through. They also had to confront the organization's myriad stakeholders—some of which could be resistant to change—asking them to also face the current realities, investigate and learn about the different viewpoints that emerged, and be open to the new ideas that offered the possibilities for finding the right solution. Each reinvention of the organization reflects a deeper exploration and understanding of the right problem to be solved.

For the Hunger Project, to create such a change in mindset requires the attribute of curious confrontation. Throughout our research we found this attribute to be consistently present. Though we can safely say that it isn't 100 percent of the time present in how things get done, it almost always exists when people are applying design thinking to a problem. And, it is especially valuable when design thinking is used to confront differing viewpoints and conflicts. In light of this, we decided to name this attribute and, as best as we could, give it a definition. We eventually landed on "Curious Confrontation," which we define as *facing differing ideas and mindsets with the desire to investigate and learn.*

DESIGN THINKING AS A CONFRONTATION TOOL

One of the culture keys, and a cornerstone to how people interpret culture, is how disagreement and conflict are managed. It has a great deal to do with how people feel safe in a culture, including their experience of what is acceptable and safe behavior, and what is considered unacceptable and unsafe. More than at any other moment in time, people learn about the culture they're in when they experience conflict. One of questions that we asked, which wound up providing us one of the key attributes consistent across our study group organizations, focused on the influence that the use of design thinking has on

CURIOUS CONFRONTATION:
Facing differing ideas and mindsets with the desire to investigate and learn.

how people manage disagreement and conflict. We ended up with a set of insights, with five that stood out as being the most significant:

1. Design thinking provides an effective tool for confronting and managing disagreement and conflict.
2. Organizations using design thinking have a belief in and positive mindset about curiosity.
3. People who use design thinking demonstrate better inquiry and listening skills, which is key in managing disagreement and conflict effectively.
4. Because design thinking skills can be applied to dealing with disagreement and conflict, confrontation happens in a more timely and healthier manner, thereby avoiding much of the dysfunction and consequences associated with it.
5. Design thinking is a valued process for confronting disagreements and misalignments among functions, and their leaders, and effectively breaking down unhealthy silos.

It's worth repeating that one of the greatest challenges any organization or team will face lies in how it effectively manages disagreement and conflict. The advantage the organizations in our study group have is that the process of design thinking creates a platform for the constructive management of diverse thinking and strategies, and the conflict that often naturally results. Viewing disagreement and conflict as an opportunity is a quality design thinking organizations can engage in. It's an aspect of creativity and innovation that is natural to any environment in which people are committed to finding and creating the best solutions possible.

In some cases, this commitment results in competition among teams or groups in an organization. When managed properly as part of an organization's culture, such competitive creativity can be leveraged as a means to drive more innovative solutions to market. When teams compete

> One of the greatest challenges any organization or team will face is how it effectively manages disagreement and conflict.

with one another, it can also add to the speed at which innovation takes place. A good example of such an environment is at some of the Samsung R&D centers. Here, several design thinking teams are established to work on the same challenges, at the same time. The teams work independently, don't communicate with one another, and often don't even know about the work of other teams. Their goal is to use design thinking to discover new products and services needs and solutions within a specific domain. This does not appear to be a case of lack of management coordination, but rather a case of putting more resources into solving a given problem area to increase the probability of success. In this environment, internal design thinking team competitiveness is encouraged, and it seems quite practical in that corporate culture. This may be one of the reasons Samsung innovation seems to be far outpacing Apple innovation in recent years. Although internally competing groups and teams—when clearly articulated as part of an organization's culture and led in a healthy manner—can provide a great benefit, it can also backfire, leading to a lack of information sharing and unwarranted redundancy and duplication. It can also result in a more critical win-lose environment or the bringing to market of products not fully realized. Despite some hiccups along the way, Samsung has used this approach with a great deal of success.

DEVELOPING CONFLICT-MANAGEMENT SKILLS

As leaders show a willingness to support the teaching of design thinking skills to their employees, they soon become aware of the benefit they get from its use as a conflict management tool. This includes paying more attention to the development of communication and conflict skills that support its success. Because design thinking is a way of leading with curiosity, it encourages embracing ambiguity, uncertainty, and confusion. In doing so, people come to understand the value of listening to one another, allowing for the creative process of building one idea upon another. It also feeds the ability of people to move from a reliance on individual creativity and contribution, to behaving more collaboratively and engaging in shared creativity. It all leads back to the understanding that an openness to listening to one another results in improved levels of inquiry, a necessary element in effectively and resolving conflict.

The skills of listening and seeking understanding are key to empathy, the first step in the design thinking process. Genuine inquiry and open listening are paramount for users of design thinking to be successful and, as the result of lessened levels of fear, leads to the increased levels of emotional maturity and safety that directly impact how conflict is constructively managed. The result of lesser levels of fear translates into the free expression that leads to the ability of people to engage in the idea generation that feeds the process of co-creation. When applied to conflicts, design thinking results in greater openness and faster generation of ideas, better feedback loops, and less competition over whose idea is better.

A MINDSET OF CURIOSITY

There's an old saying that curiosity killed the cat. Of course, there's no scientific evidence that this is true. Nor is there evidence that a cat has nine lives. There *is* evidence that people with a greater degree of curiosity are more inquisitive, are more open to new experiences, and generate more original ideas.

Evidence also indicates that a sense of curiosity is a characteristic of genius. Most notably, what is called one's curiosity quotient (CQ) is a critical contributor to one's level of social intelligence. Research shows that curious people have more friends, have more significant relationships, and are viewed by others more highly. In light of their increased ability to be more inquiring, others see them as more considerate, interested, and empathetic. As a result, they are seen as more likable. Lastly, research indicates that people who are curious are happier, healthier, and more productive, and have better social relationships.

Research indicates that people who are curious are happier, healthier, and more productive, and have better social relationships.

Before you go off to reinvent your hiring practices, we want to be clear that we're not making the suggestion that you re-strategize your recruiting and hiring practices (though after reading this chapter, you may want to). We're simply pointing out that when it comes to managing disagreement and conflict, people who demonstrate curiosity are more likely to engage in curious confrontation and, in appreciation of non-conformist thinking, tend to be more open to looking at problems in different ways and seeking new solutions and ideas. We would even go so far as to say that curiosity is a form of intelligence.

The origin of this idea goes back to the expanding definition of what a mindset is. Originally it was defined as a way of thinking, held by a group of people, that is so established that it prevents change. In business, we typically refer to this as a paradigm. In 2006, Carol Dweck introduced another lens on mindset, creating a differentiation between what she called a "fixed" mindset and a "growth" mindset. She focused her thinking on the individual and defined a fixed mindset as one in which people believe their basic abilities, intelligence, and talents are fixed traits. She defined the growth mindset as one in which people believe that their talents and abilities can be developed and that they can learn and become smarter. In simplifying these ideas, people often refer to them as more open or closed-minded.[1]

In a taking a more scientific approach, in a 2014 *Harvard Business Review* article, Tomas Chamorro-Premuzic related curiosity to intelligence and emotional intelligence. Chamorro-Premuzic compared CQ (curiosity quotient) to IQ (intelligence quotient: mental ability) and EQ (emotional quotient: emotional intelligence), stating that people with higher CQ are more inquisitive and open to new experiences. Furthermore, according to Chamorro-Premuzic, there's evidence that when it comes to managing complexity, individuals with higher CQ are generally more tolerant of ambiguity and that CQ leads to higher levels of intellectual investment and knowledge acquisition, especially in science and art. He also states that, like EQ, CQ can be developed.[2]

This leads us to a very important conclusion that we find consistent with our research findings: As an organization invests in training its people in design thinking, it's developing and affecting its cultural curiosity mindset. The result can be seen in the development of better listening skills, improved openness to new ideas that lead to innovation, greater empathy, decreased self-censoring, and higher levels of openness and free expression. These are all traits that we associate with the improved management of disagreement and conflict, and the attribute of curious confrontation.

It is also apparent that, as an attribute of design thinking organizations, curious confrontation has a direct influence on how people perceive the culture of the organization. Because the way disagreement and conflict are managed is such a significant aspect of how people experience a culture, it is clear that as an organization develops its attribute of curious confrontation, it increases its capability to innovate. It also allows for the further application of design thinking as a key ingredient in the intentional design of the organization's ideal culture.

What are some of the ways in which organizations can better leverage it to manage disagreement and conflict more effectively and, by doing so, move toward greater levels of innovation? Here are some examples:

- *Keep the customer first.* Keeping a focus on the customer creates a shared understanding and alignment to the intended outcome. Asking "What are we are here for?" and "Why is this important?" reminds everyone involved why the conflict likely exists and what everyone's shared intention is. Often overlooked is how this can also apply to the management of customers, particularly in a business-to-business relationship.
- *Always critique the work.* Giving and receiving feedback isn't always easy, especially considering that people can quickly fall into defensive modes of behavior and feel ill at ease. One of the core operating principles at PIXAR is to always critique the work. This even means to look at the work during critique, not the artist that created it. The principle should be used for design thinking groups as well. Because design thinking is focused on empathy, insight, rapid ideation, and immediate feedback, there is typically a greater degree of focus on making the process work than on criticizing or unfairly questioning someone's contribution. Regardless, it's good to be aware of the

possible disagreement and conflict, and be ready to bring
the focus back to the problem that everyone is trying to
solve. This is particularly true when design thinking is
being used to address a specific conflict area.

- *Trust in the process.* First and foremost, trust in the process of using empathy and inquiry with intention. One
  way to use design thinking for better managing conflict
  and decision-making is to create a process specific to
  it. As you can imagine, depending on the culture, this
  can result in some fairly innovative approaches. As an
  example, at AMP the finance department uses evidence
  of a focus on improving customer experience in making
  decisions as to what budget requests to approve. They
  require teams to use design thinking to support their
  budget requests. The intention is to not focus on any one
  individual or department budget desires, but rather to
  have the process show evidence of an improved customer
  experience as an outcome.

- *Ask simple, yet critical questions.* Using design thinking as a framework not only increases the capability of
  people to listen, it also helps develop their inquiry skills.
  We found many great examples of how design thinking
  led to the reframing of difficult questions and provided
  framework for finding the critical and simple questions
  to ask that move people toward finding simple and powerful solutions. One of the most powerful questions to
  ask is "What's missing?" Conflict is a signal that a need
  or desire is going unmet—that there is a gap between
  what people have and what they want—so this is the
  most direct and empathetic question to ask. What's missing: *for the customer, in our communication, in our relationship, in how we're working, that led to the problem,
  for you?* It can be applied well to virtually any situation.
  Other good questions to consider using include:
  — What is our shared desired outcome?
  — What is our intention for the relationship?

— How can we look at this in a new way or from a different viewpoint?
— How can we better understand what each party is asking for?
— What will we change about our interaction to achieve better results?
— How can we use what we already have in a new way?
— What change can we make to create something entirely new?
— What do we stop doing that gets in our way?
— Who do we need to include and get involved?

In moments of disagreement and conflict, the use of critical questioning helps in identifying the underlying problem that needs to be solved and can be quite powerful in opening the door to open dialogue and the resolution of conflicts.

- *Emphasize your purpose and intention.* At Johnson & Johnson, the company's principles are front and center, and guide more than the design and innovation of its products. When there is disagreement or conflict, or there is need for a difficult conversation, people rely on the principles for guidance and exploring what the right thing to do is. Having an anchor in an organization's purpose and values can lead to the identification of the real problem or how the real problem can be resolved.

- *Come from a place of inquiry.* Rather than being tellers, design thinkers are explorers. They ask questions and listen fearlessly to the answers they receive. It's important to keep this at the forefront, especially when it comes to disagreement and conflict. That being said, in the heat of the moment, regardless of how good one's intention, things can go sideways. For that reason, it's worth noting that giving one another permission to give and receive feedback is key. Even better is to be able to ask for it and openly receive it. Using the communication skills associated with design thinking not only helps to frame the

real problem, it allows for the dialogue necessary to find
the right solution.

- *Act aligned.* As we share in Chapter 14, the alignment of
  leadership behavior is a key to success. In our research
  we also came across some examples of misaligned leadership, resulting in mixed messages and a loss of trust in
  the application of design thinking and its use in dealing
  with conflict. It's important for leaders to not avoid disagreement or conflict, not listen well, or not confront the
  key problems and questions necessary to success. Rather,
  leaders should role-model and reinforce the use of design
  thinking and demonstrate curious confrontation.

- *Measure results.* One of the best ways to measure the
  results of curious confrontation is to track and measure
  the impact of the healthy and constructive management
  of disagreement and conflict to the actual performance
  outcomes. In conversation after conversation, the people
  in our study group organizations pointed to specific
  events that led to higher levels of innovation and performance. Oftentimes, the conflict an organization faced
  required the ability to be truthful and constructive in
  managing it. Tracking events, the outcomes reached
  by the creative and constructive management of them,
  and their resulting performance outcomes reinforces
  the desired behaviors that help embed the use of design
  thinking skills in a culture.

- *Leverage breadth and depth.* Great design thinking recognizes the need for involvement. Relying solely on depth
  of knowledge and insight, or a specific expertise, may
  result in the exclusion of people that may have insights
  valuable to understanding a problem or have good ideas
  to contribute in finding the right solution. Conversely,
  just because more people are involved in trying to solve a
  problem doesn't mean that the right people are involved.
  Because design thinking requires consideration of both
  factors, when it comes to difficult situations, conflicts

that all too often are affected by defensive behaviors, including intentional exclusion, it reminds people to be more open as to who needs to be involved.

- *Leaders need to take action.* What most often keeps leaders from confronting disagreement and conflict is the fear of being incompetent and not having the ability to get to the right solution, or not being able to achieve the outcome they want. Fortunately, design thinking provides a path to competency whereby leaders can have a sense of predictability in and that they can use as a communication framework to be more successful. This is not only a benefit to leaders. It is a benefit to the cultures they lead in. More than any other time, the value of role-modeling and reinforcement is front and center when conflict is at hand. How a leader behaves in such situations is critical.

In our research we found that, for the most part, people have a positive perception of design thinking and the constructive nature of how it influences how people work together. We also came across the reality that regardless of the methodology that an organization and its leadership applies to creating change, disagreement and conflict will naturally be a part of the change process. We also learned that the simple idea of using design thinking to manage disagreement and conflict is not always recognized. Yet, the tenets of design thinking align to those that we associate with conflict resolution, and the collaboration necessary to focus and find innovative resolutions that deliver meaningful results.

The advantage of design thinking is how empathetic listening and the creation of a shared understanding of differing perspectives set the stage for collaboration and problem-solving. Sometimes the solution to a conflict isn't perfect the first time around. This is particularly true in dealing with conflicts within teams and the larger context of the organization. Understanding this allows for an appreciation of the idea that, like any solution, resolutions and agreements to conflicts need also to be tested. And, if necessary, they can also be improved upon.

Lastly, one thing that is clear throughout the organizations in our study is that, when applied, the value of design thinking is a reliable means through which to develop the skills necessary for the curious confrontation—a means of effectively managing disagreement, conflict, and the host of assorted challenges and issues organizations, at all levels, must deal with. What is also true is that the better trained and skilled people are in use of design thinking, the more they are able to rely on it as an effective conflict management tool. This is likely one of the more hidden benefits of why the organizations in our study have scaled design thinking (see the chart in Chapter 6) at the levels they have. The powerful lesson? Train everyone.

Design thinking manifests the curious confrontation that helps them in overcoming one of the aspects of culture that organizations struggle with most—disagreement and conflict—turning it from a disadvantage into an innovation advantage. Curious confrontation accelerates the power of the collective imagination.

Co-Creation

"Two heads are better than one."
—John Heywood

The organizations in our research are not bound by the limitations of their structure or the defined roles people find themselves in. Rather, they invite inclusion, and bring together diverse groups and parties to collaboratively produce mutually benefitting and jointly valued outcomes. Both internally and externally, they deliberately engage people in the act of co-creation, eventually making it a key attribute of their innovative cultures.

The idea of co-creation is not a new concept. In its first forms, it focused on bringing together broader groups of consumers and customers, thereby enabling the provider of a product or service to generate new ideas. It offered a means of bringing together different parties to produce a mutually benefitting outcome. Over time, this resulted in an increased appreciation of the value of understanding the unique experiences and perspectives of customers. What followed were the acknowledgment and use of co-creation in innovatively thinking about business strategies, structures, systems, and eventually, organizational cultures. Throughout this book, there are examples of how organizations use the pull factor to multiply the engagement of the variety of contributors to their design thinking processes.

THE PHILIPS STORY

One of the powerful examples of what happens when an organization takes the idea of co-creation and expands the process to a broader set of participants and applications is Philips, the Dutch technology company that, through its divisions, now focuses its innovation in the areas of health and wellness technology. Sean Carney is the chief design officer of Royal Philips and is responsible for building the design thinking capabilities throughout the Philips organization. He told us that, much like the other innovative organizations in our study, Philips created a branding for their design thinking process. In the spirit of greater involvement, they call their program the Co-Create process framework. It's an embedded component and competency within the company that is forwarded through a company-wide training program and that is part of Philips University and the Philips Business process framework.

Sean joined Philips in 2011, succeeding Philip's design leader Stephano Marzano. Sean arrived at a time when the company needed to create a shift in its broader business strategy. Over Marzano's two decades of influence, and following the pioneering design leadership path set by Robert Blaich, Philips had become a design powerhouse and the envy of the product design world. During Marzano's tenure, Philips Design operated as an internal service provider to the various divisions of the electronics giant, operating essentially as a design agency within the larger organization. Now the company needed more: a broader and more integrated use of design thinking that would also influence the company's business strategy.

Under Sean's leadership, design has been integrated as a strategy and a practice throughout Philips, contributing to the transformation of the company from being a consumer electronics product and lighting company, into a focused leader in health technology. This is a dramatic strategic shift, and is coupled with how design thinking is now used in the company and its influence on how the company focuses its innovation capability.

The change in separating health technology and lighting also helped move the company from a financial under-performance in 2011 to a return to delivering higher financial returns. According to the Philips Annual Report, in 2016 the company's net income more than doubled (to €1.5 billion, or $1.8 billion USD) from the previous year and its income from operations increased from €1.0 billion to €1.9 billion, the equivalent of an increase from approximately $1.2 to $2.27 billion USD.[1] As is often the case, though design thinking is credited with the creation of powerful innovation in products and services, it is also a key contributor to the creation of innovative organizational strategies that result in financial outcomes. As is so often the case with strategies that fall into the realm of human resources and organizational development, and that are difficult to track in terms of ROI and measurable financial value, the results at Philips (as well as other of our case study examples) demonstrate a more-than-significant effect on the financial bottom line. And, as some of the case studies in this book demonstrate, design thinking is also a key contributor to organizational transformations that get greater financial results.

Ferdy Gilsing is now an associate director of design in the BMW Group. Prior to taking on his new role at BMW, Ferdy was working in Sean Carney's organization at Philips and helped develop the Co-Create program. Ferdy shared with us that the program was designed to unleash the creative potential within Philips to develop meaningful, people-centered innovation, by embedding the principles and mindsets of design thinking into the organization.

A key to success in engaging the various groups in the co-creation strategy was recognizing the need to position the training in the Philips Academy, thereby allowing it to be scaled throughout the organization. At that time, HR was building a Philips Academy, and the principles of design thinking fit perfectly into that curriculum. Frans van Houten, the CEO of Philips, who was very intrigued about the use and influence of design thinking, assured that the Academy would receive the proper funding. Design and HR worked together to ensure that design thinking was developed and implemented in the organization properly. The result was the establishment of a "10%–20%–70%" training model—that is, 10 percent of the design thinking team became moderators and co-create leaders, 20 percent of the team acted as coaches, and 70 percent of the team actively focused on the principle of learning by doing, and co-creating with people internal and external to the company.

Important to the successful and meaningful implementation was that the training was applied on real-life challenges, mainly in the healthcare domain. The different types of challenges varied in the areas of innovation for business strategy, new value propositions, business transformation, and customer engagements. Design thinking was used to reframe the challenge of how to compete in the sector and to come up with a shared vision from which both internal groups and external partners and stakeholders could explore possible strategies and value propositions. By working on real-life business challenges, the Co-Create program delivered measurable impact and achieved sustainable change for the organization in the transformation of moving from a product company into a healthcare solutions provider.

INSIDE OUT

Innovative organizations display an ability to manifest the belief that the more open they are internally, within their own organizations, the more they are able to be open and engage externally. This results in the capability to involve a much broader group of players and contributors to the innovation process. It also allows the leveraging of co-creation, which results in greater levels of information-sharing, more timely and productive problem-solving, and better-informed employees, customers, and leadership—not to mention higher levels of engagement and loyalty among those involved. In support of co-creation, there is also the sharing of knowledge with, and training of, groups and individuals that are typically ignored or excluded. Without design thinking and co-creation, these assets commonly go unrecognized and unused. Yet, in design thinking cultures, these oft-hidden assets are the powerful source of the creative influence that results in great innovations. Design thinking organizations lead with creativity.

Not lost on designers and design thinkers, this value was soon applied not only in better understanding customers, but it soon found its way to being applied internally, with employees and groups in and across organizations, and beyond. Now, the idea of co-creation is being applied to the expansive network that any organization is connected to, including its vendors, outsourced services, partners, and the variety of current and potential product and service users. For non-profits, it can also include donors. The intended outcomes are the increases in communication, connection, pursuit of knowledge, and open idea-sharing that result in increased innovation and value. Co-creation is an attribute that engages and leverages the three pillars of the collective imagination.

> Co-creation is an attribute that engages and leverages the three pillars of the collective imagination.

The key to success in co-creation—whether it relates to a product or service or one's role in a company—is the understanding that individuals have unique emotional experiences that personalize their participation. This ability to personalize it creates the opportunity for the use of empathy and understanding, which results in the appreciation of the emotional (or feelings) aspect of that experience. Communicating and sharing the emotional quality provides the fuel for the generating of multiple ideas—ideas that can, very quickly, end up delivering greater levels of innovation. An aspect of arriving at success requires organizations to think expansively and more inclusively.

To get the most of co-creation requires a strategic approach as to how to implement and use design thinking. Although the pull factor and the desire of people to want to be included are natural aspects of design thinking, left to its organic development, it will most often fall short of its true potential. Going back to our look at Philips, and as Sean Carney told us, at the outset there were a lot of enlightened people at Philips who had read about design thinking in places like the *Harvard Business Review (HBR)* and wanted to engage the methods for problem-solving. From executives to individual contributors there was a ground swell of interest, including many of the 400 designers in his organization. Many people wanted to engage with design thinking, yet for it to really gain traction and scale, it had to be well coordinated and organized.

With the intention to embed a high amount of design thinking company-wide, Sean decided to engage with a business transition team. As a result, they trained a handful of designers to go out and work with other groups to apply design thinking and to facilitate design thinking sessions. They started with a team of just five or six people trained as expert design thinking trainers, then it grew to 15 people, then about 50, and now they have about 150 expert-level trainers available to drop in and help any department that needs it. The broadening and scaling of design thinking increased involvement; it also resulted in the ability to invite more and more people to co-create together. Of great significance is that the broader strategic effort resulted in the inclusion of the entire executive team, coupled with customers, insurers, and healthcare authorities around the world, to use design thinking to co-create and envision future propositions for healthcare. As an outcome for Philips, these initiatives have led to billions of dollars in sales over the last few years. In light of these co-creation successes, design thinking sessions are now written into the sales process and are part of the long-term engagements with their clients, appropriately called Bootcamps.

Here is an example of the Bootcamp process in action. It began with training 200 people in their sales organization in China in how to use design thinking and co-creation techniques with their customers. The view is that engaging the sales organization with design thinking makes so much sense because salespeople generally have empathy for their customers and like to discover customer problems so they can help solve them, so it comes natural. In the workshop, they put the product catalogs and sales lists away, sat down with customers, and focused on understanding their problems, the day-to-day realities and challenges that they face, and envisioning opportunities and future possibilities. This is very energizing for the sales organization and their customers, and has created a number of significant outcomes. For example, the Philips salespeople helped one of their customers look at problems as broad as the impacts of future city planning and growth, and what impacts they may have on their small local hospital and primary-care facilities.

Sean shared with us that they believe the use of design thinking is changing the culture at Philips in many ways. It's increasing empathy internally and externally, expanding the involvement of customers and end users in new solutions, and it's helping to solve much bigger problems—systems problems that have multiple owners. This all involves greater collaboration and open-minded people to help create better solutions both internally and for customer products and services.

OUTSIDE IN

Examples of co-creation are also evident in external partners working from the outside in. Though most design and consulting firm engagements seem to come and go, with a merry-go-round of clients, probably the most amazing co-creation story is with Teague and Boeing. Seattle-based design firm Teague has designed nearly every Boeing aircraft interior since the 1940s, from the post–WWII Stratocruiser to the most recent 787 Dreamliner. Teague is the oldest design firm in America, founded in 1926 by industrial designer, illustrator, and architect Walter Darwin Teague, and has taken the notion of co-creation to new levels. More than 200 Teague employees work in a Teague design studio located inside a gigantic Boeing building in Everett, Washington, working alongside Boeing employees on a daily basis. Teague employees worked very closely with Boeing employees to help co-create the 787 Dreamliner interior design. That aircraft has noticeably larger windows, and a cabin environment that is measurably more comfortable and an improved flight experience for passengers. The 787 Dreamliner is the most successful commercial airplane launch in the history of commercial aviation, with nearly 1,200 orders valued at more than $190 billion.

When we talked with Frog Design about co-creation, we learned that design thinking is embedded in their new employee orientation, and they have an ongoing internal employee training practice about design thinking called Participatory Design. Industrial designer Hartmut

Esslinger, who, starting with the Apple IIc, designed the first comput-
ers for Steve Jobs, founded Frog in 1969. Today the firm invites clients
to work with them inside their studios to co-create new products and
services.

Much like Teague and Frog, design firm IDEO, a relative young-
ster founded in 1991, has significantly popularized and advanced
the methods of design thinking and is committed to embedding
co-creating into their culture. A *Harvard Business Review* article
describes IDEO as having a culture of helping, or a spirit of helpfulness.[2] This helpfulness can be used in problem-solving and facili-
tating all manner of co-creation. In this situation, the *HBR* authors
suggest leaders express their participation by both giving and seeking help themselves. This tends to level the playing field, from
C-suite to individual contributor, encourages knowledge-sharing
and co-creation, and taps into the creative intelligence of all. You
may be thinking, *Our company is not a Teague, Frog, or IDEO*, but
we suggest that maybe it is. Like the consultancies, your organization is full of knowledge workers trying to solve complex problems. Your challenge is simply to make creativity and co-creation,
through the means of design thinking, a core part of your employee
behavior as well.

PROCESS ALIGNMENTS

From our research we found that one of the ways co-creation supports design thinking is through the multiple ways in which it is syn-
ergistic with, and can be aligned with, other processes and systems
for improvement and innovation. This includes the variety of processes used across an organization's various functions. As an example,
at Philips, the chief of HR ran a three-day design thinking session
aimed at designing improvements in HR. Although several valuable
solutions emerged, they also realized that the Co-Create framework
comes quite natural to HR organizations. In fact, they had been practicing some of the methods of design thinking, such as contextual
inquiry and the use of pilot testing new ideas and strategies with
small groups of employees, for years.

This led to the discovery that a key reason why the use of design thinking is growing so rapidly at Philips, is it has traction that comes from the ability to align its use with other processes, such as Agile, Agile Enterprise, and Lean. The basic principles of Agile and Lean, sprints and design thinking, combined are very powerful together. Design thinking is also now part of the Philips stage-gate process as well, and is engaged at the very front end of just about every project. At the onset of each project, development teams are tasked with creating a value proposition statement, which involves articulating user value and building a business case. This is how design is now helping lead business transformation teams across the entire organization, using their Innovation to Market Process (I to P Excellence), of which design thinking is at the core.

In a similar vein, Visa has a program called Design Hack Practice. Every month they put their learning into practice and how to apply it to solve fundamental claims problems both at Visa and within client teams. Recently they ran a design hack program in Vietnam, Indonesia, and the Philippines to create solutions for a bank. The chairman of the bank took part in the hack, which resulted in finding ways to solve some end-user problems by using Visa services and thinking methods in their product innovation portfolio with their customers. Programs like this design thinking approach to hacks build tangible business results.

According to Kevin Lee, Visa's global head of design, who we introduced you to earlier, more profound is the impact on the ground level. The company is delivering organizational strategies by helping everybody understand the importance of empathy, listening skills, synthesizing, conceptualizing ideas, and involving the user experience. What's so impactful is that they are solving local problems on a global basis, not just those that are American-based. As an example, in support of leveraging co-creation, they ran a two-day design hack with more than 70 people co-located in Singapore and Berlin.

The intent of Day 1 is to have multiple sprints and empathy interviews, involving end users. The teams synthesize, state problem statements, identify requirements, and sketch out everything on whiteboards. On Day 2, they revisited Day 1 findings, reviewed all the concepts, and selected the concept to move forward; and each group created and gave a two-minute pitch of their story. A team of expert judges reviewed and selected the winner.

Another powerful example of a successful result is Visa's success with Costco. For years Costco had been using the American Express card with their members. When Costco sent out an open bid for proposals, rather than bidding by price, Visa used its design thinking program to create an innovation story. They helped Costco imagine a new two-year vision and made a short video bringing the vision to life. This vision of innovation and a new future customer experience was a key element to their proposal, and Costco selected Visa. Surpassing American Express, and using design thinking with the sales organization in creating the proposal, was an impactful win.

Kevin points out that all of this is definitely having a positive impact on Visa's culture. People get intensely involved, and design thinking is not slow; it can be done fast. It can also be very precise and have a high return on the minimum investment. It gives people confidence, empowers people, and it helps people learn. Kevin told us that people say "I can do this, too." It's so much more engaging and powerful than having a team put together a PowerPoint deck. And, as the question may have already crossed your mind, at Visa, there are no monetary rewards for participating in design thinking and co-creation. It's the natural pull factor in play, internally and externally multiplying engagement, and transforming the company's workforce.

Lastly, through the co-creation process, Visa's customers are happy to be engaged in the human part of the work. Like several of the organizations in our case study, Visa has built innovation centers in different parts of the world. Thus far, they have open innovation labs in San Francisco, London, Dubai, Singapore, and in 2017 the plans call for Berlin and Sydney to come on line. At the centers, customers will have access to designers, design thinkers, and businesspeople in these labs to co-create with, as well as access to their expertise.

Of the members of our study group, most have some form of innovation center or lab. Several, including SAP, GE, Kaiser Permanente, Intuit, and Marriott, have innovation centers in which customers and other people can participate. The creation of such open spaces for co-creation is a part of the dedication to using design thinking to create greater levels of innovation. At the very core is a commitment to creating engagements with the customers and providing them with an actual experience, one that leads to shared innovative solutions. It's human-centered design; it's human working. Customers, too, are feeling the effect of the pull factor.

12

Open Spaces

*"We are never more fully alive, more
completely ourselves, or more deeply engrossed
in anything than when we are playing."*
—Charles Schaefer

One morning while running a workshop at Autodesk in San Francisco, Thomas noticed people walking through the building with pushcarts filled with markers, sticky notes, colored paper, scissors, snacks, and all kinds of fun artwork paraphernalia. As they made their way through the building, the employees pushing the carts replenished the variety of work areas and conference rooms with the ingredients and tools that would be used in collaborative work sessions that would take place in different parts of the building as the day unfolded. *Beautiful,* he thought.

Autodesk is an American multinational software corporation that makes digital tools for the architecture, engineering, construction, design, manufacturing, media, and entertainment industries. Tom found the physical space at Autodesk extremely effective for design thinking work and collaboration. Over the course of several years, the space that people work in at Autodesk has been transformed to directly mirror the company-wide commitment to design thinking and making it a part of their corporate culture. As such, it also made a commitment to redesign physical workspaces, providing for an integrated combination of private offices, private workstations, shared workstations, and open workspaces for breakout sessions—spaces that express a sense of playfulness and through which one can see fascinating interior and environmental design strategies being applied.

In particular, Tom noticed that the conference rooms are very effectively designed. Of course they are fully wired, with projectors, whiteboards, and all of the things you would expect in a creative design thinking organization. To facilitate creative thinking and interaction, the conference rooms are furnished with mobile furnishings. Chairs are of different heights, including bar stools that facilitate an easier transition from standing to sitting, especially welcome to people who do their creative thinking on their feet. Throughout the offices, workstations are height-adjustable, allowing people to raise and lower their height to sit and stand as they please. Whiteboards are available throughout the office so that ideas, comments, drawings, and different creative expressions can be shared and built upon.

At Autodesk, the layout of conference rooms and workstations is inside-out. In other words, rather than workstations being placed at the center of the building and conference rooms and manager offices lining the parameter and windows, the conference rooms and offices are at the center, and employee workstations line the windows and outer areas of the floor plan. Throughout the past two decades, multiple studies have been conducted on the effects of light and nature on human creativity and problem-solving. People in environments with plants, natural light, and better views not only perform better, they also experience less stress. At this Autodesk location, the space most conducive to personal well-being and collaboration is occupied by the staff, not by those seeking the corner office.

Other experiments show that open environments not only increase the potential for increased levels of communication, they also tend to generate moderate noise levels. Whereas silence is preferred for some types of work, people working in environments with moderate noise levels are more likely to work at increased levels of creativity, as well as be more productive and be less distracted than those working in high noise environments. This supports Autodesk's approach to offering their people to work in a multitude of environments supporting both individual preference as well as the capability to engage with others in a number of different ways.

LEGO'S TRANSFORMATIONAL SPACES

LEGO doesn't talk very much about design thinking. However, when you explore inside LEGO you will find design thinking used throughout their entire operation. We think it's safe to say that human-centered design is strongly embedded in their participation and community-oriented culture. It's every bit about how the company operates. Evidence of this is LEGO's commitment to co-creation with end users, to human centered design practices, and to design as an integrated element in everything they do.[1]

Looking to the future, LEGO's new office, set to open in September 2017 in Billund, Denmark, will likely become a model for other organizations to follow. Why? For starters, it is created to provide the sense of community that aligns to LEGO's approach to market and one of their core business strategies to nurture the worldwide community loyal to their product and brand. Secondly, in alignment to culture, the design has a list of features that creates open space for collaboration and a sense of freedom to work in a manner that breaks down structure, bureaucracy, and creative limitations.

Here is a short list of some of the work environment elements consistent with the company's emphasis on creative play: a green roof garden, play areas, lounge areas, a mini golf course, informal meeting areas, hot desks, green courtyards, and temporary workstations—all of which are wrapped in a structure that has the appearance of, and is designed in the manner of the product itself: LEGO bricks. To bring nature and well-being into the environment, the design of the building allows for a generous flow of daylight, giving it a sense of openness. This is all consistent with the design that speaks to the creative design capability embedded in its culture.[2]

"It is the LEGO philosophy that 'good quality play' enriches a child's life—and lays the foundation for later adult life. We believe that play is a key element in children's growth and development and stimulates the imagination and the emergence of ideas and creative expression. All LEGO products are based on this underlying philosophy of learning and development through play."
—LEGO (from *leg godt*: "play well")

Even today, as one might imagine, the LEGO headquarters looks a bit like a LEGOLAND, with atrium-style seating areas stacked like LEGO bricks and creative play areas. Lego has about 300 designers and a very sophisticated system of design management is integrated into their playful culture. The designers at LEGO work in five large, shared atriums, each with a unique theme that coincides with how people use their products. The designers from different product areas use these spaces and are inspired by the artifacts in them. One design director of LEGO told us that design is so integrated at LEGO that it's running the show. Though this may be a bit of a stretch, it's apparent that design and creativity are integral to the LEGO business model, their space, and their corporate culture. Design influences how people work together both professionally and in physical proximity.

CREATIVE SPACES

At the organizational and team levels, the use of design thinking requires creativity by the participants and, to its benefit, the right corporate or team environment. This includes what collaboration and communities, local and virtual, look like, and how they inform and reinforce creative expression, behavior, and open communication. In addition to open-mindedness and acceptance, open, inviting, and stimulating physical spaces that allow for interaction, gathering, and community are essential ingredients to success. We discovered that such environments do not place restrictions on participation. Rather, in a variety of forms spanning from open community spaces to more organized design labs, they are appealing, invite participation, support open brainstorming, and often offer engagement in forms of artistic expression. Through the use of various forms of technology, the aspects of open space are also applied to the creation of virtual open spaces, allowing for a multiplying effect and expanding of engagement.

A common attribute of highly innovative cultures is the attention paid to creating an environment that promotes expansive and creative thinking. This includes what physical space looks and feels like, how virtual communities and teams use visual tools and technologies, and their effect and reinforcement of creative and collaborative behavior and open communication. When workspaces and virtual communities are more engaging and creatively stimulating, with more capability and opportunity for employees and team members to gather, collaborate, and create together, it invokes the natural processes of the collective imagination, visual reasoning, and mind mapping. The attribute of open spaces is a means of the emotional expression that invites creative expression and more open and energized dialogue. An aspect of strategically leveraging the attribute of open spaces is to think creatively about the use of space, technology, visual tools, and eventually the application of different forms of art.

> "Play is the only way the highest intelligence of humankind can unfold."
> —Joseph Chilton Pearce

ARTIFACTS OF INNOVATION

LEGO's first and perhaps most timeless innovation is the creation of the Automatic Binding Bricks in 1949, the forerunner to the LEGO bricks of today, invented in 1959. Often, building with LEGO bricks is described as magical, taking adults back to childhood, and releasing the uninhibited ability to play, to imagination as they did as youngsters. The creativity required for the open-minded and free expression required for the attainment of higher levels of innovation is the key ingredient of play. LEGO calls it "laying the foundation for later adult life."

Today, LEGO is used by organizations worldwide in training workshops, leadership development seminars, large conferences, and the like, to invite participants and attendees to have fun and think creatively. Edgar and Thomas have attended and spoken at a number of conferences and team-building events at which attendees are provided with a package of LEGO stuff. Often, the first thing people do is start playing with it, or collaborating with one another and manifesting ideas on what can be built when everyone starts sharing their pieces with one another.

According to LEGO, "When children play, they develop vital skills. We are providers of fun, engaging and creative play experiences that help children develop social, emotional and intellectual skills, laying a foundation that lasts a lifetime. The LEGO® System in Play is unique in that it combines structure, logic and creativity, which enables learning through play by reasoning systematically and thinking creatively."[3] These are capabilities that any organization wants its members to have. They are skills that, according to many of those we interviewed, are not always easy to find. They are also employee and leadership attributes required for, and developed in the use of, design thinking.

Like many organizations, LEGO's work environment is filled with cultural and product artifacts. In of itself, the new Billund office building is an artifact, designed in the manner and with the appearance of LEGO bricks. From a distance, the building evokes the playful and creative aspects of *why* the company exists and is a part of its *how*. It also conveys the ideals and purpose of the organization, and is clear messaging of its mission ("to inspire and develop the builders of tomorrow").

Cultural artifacts are important to the space that people work in, not only because they are evidence of the accomplishments of the enterprise. They are also symbols and emotional reminders of the purpose that led to their creation, and that is tied to the human need for it to exist. There is an emotional *why* attached to it. When one enters LEGO's offices, the artifacts are everywhere. When you enter

3M's Innovation Center, you walk into a museum of its imaginative product accomplishments. Walking into GE's Menlo Lab is walking into history. The visual identity, the shapes and forms, all evoke an emotional response as well as provide queues for the creative activity within the space.

From the perspective of innovation, artifacts represent the resolution to a problem, a conflict created by something that we want and don't have. An artifact is a response to the search for something needed to satisfy a human desire. Though the term *artifact* is now applied in a variety of ways, including to tangible by-products in software development, the most powerful use is the means through which we identify with cultural artifacts. Whether physical or virtual objects in a digital environment, they are objects created by people that inform us about the culture of the organization, and evoke the emotion associated with the collective imagination of those involved. At their best, they not only remind people of what was created, but carry with them meaning.

An organization's cultural artifacts prompt people to think about and explore why and how the objects were created. They draw emotional response. People connect to the participation, pursuit of knowledge, and free expression of creative ideas associated with the design of solutions that touches them in emotional ways. Regardless of whether they are part of the history of an organization that has been in existence for more than a century, or one in the early stages of existence, its artifacts represent its capability to innovate and are a form of creative engagement. Cultural artifacts are key elements of an organization's innovation story.

CREATING YOUR SPACE

The examples of open spaces and design of environments provided by our study group organizations offer a wealth of insight into how to create innovative surroundings for people to work and thrive in. Several organizations include innovation centers and labs that invite their customers to participate directly in, and experience the effects of, the design thinking process; examples include Visa, Deutsche

Telekom, and Marriott's interactive lab hotel. Other organizations create spaces within the organizations themselves that are supported by the experiential training of employees and other participants, such as Intuit, Autodesk, Kaiser Permanente, and SAP. We also came across a variety of examples in which organizations invited their people to participate in design thinking events in out-of-the-ordinary and unique places that stirred their creativity, evoked deep emotions, or exposed them to artifacts that connected them in more meaningful ways to their purpose and mission.

As an example, when NZTE in New Zealand brought its leaders together to design the culture of their organization, they gathered for three days at Eden Park, the home of New Zealand's All Blacks rugby team. The All Blacks are arguably the greatest team in international rugby history and are undefeated at Eden Park. A place of significant cultural pride, the site provided a deep connection to the nation's ability to innovate and compete on the global stage. Unlike gathering in a hotel meeting room, the open space looking out onto the park and its brilliant green turf, and being surrounded by artifacts of a history of success, created an ideal setting for the group's work.

While we're Down Under, let's take a short look at AMP, the leading insurance and wealth management company in Australia and New Zealand. Munib Karavdic, director, design & innovation, started their design thinking program a few years ago and has trained 700 employees on human-centered design. That's a rather impressive change for a 185-year-old insurance company. Yet times are changing. AMP does this for innovation and as a proven model to humanize its business. We could dive into our case with AMP deeply with you, but rather would like to share with you a short, interesting result of building an open creative space.

Minub started their adventure into design thinking by making a shared space for innovation. As background, the company's office space design stems around individual cubicles, small offices for managers, and generic conference rooms to share, hardly a space designed for creativity and collaboration to flourish. Minub envisioned building a culture of innovation. He transformed his small UX design department, grew it to seven service designers, and began running design thinking workshops. They soon found that they needed a larger, open space to invite people to for collaboration workshops. All he could squeeze out of the facilities department was one of the flat-out ugliest rooms at headquarters. They looked on the bright side, moved in, and transformed the space with floor to ceiling whiteboards; added moveable tables, chairs, and the appropriate tools for visualization and play; and began hosting design thinking sessions. Concurrently they created a tailored five-step design thinking process that aligns to their culture:

1. Frame the problem.
2. Understand context.
3. Define—build concepts from insights.
4. Deliver—make a minimum viable proposal.
5. Evolve—improve.

They had fun. Word spread. Within a few months it was full of people collaborating and creating. They solved wicked problems. They invited more people to join the room, and more, and began a process of training more design thinking facilitators. The CEO caught wind of this exciting initiative, and the great results it was producing, and asked Minub if he could attend a design thinking workshop. Together, they solved more significant problems and it turned into a tremendous success. As a result, the CEO called the facilities department and had his boardroom on the top floor turned into a similar open space for collaboration and creativity. He began holding his executive leadership team meetings in this space. This quickly caught on, and within a year or so, every floor of their 25-floor headquarters had an innovation lab. Now even their finance department requests proof of customer benefits and co-creation in order to approve department budgets for projects. Design thinking is also used in insurance risk assessment projects, something that previously relied only on scientific data.

Visa's innovation centers provide an experience for customers to engage in the innovation process. Retail-like environments allow for the observation and inquiry into the customer's direct experience, enhancing the ability for real-time prototyping and generating of new ideas. Far from the organization's offices in New York, the animators of the Hunger Project create experiences that reflect the geographic cultures of the areas of the world that their investors (financial donors) can be a part of. Not only does it result in an increased emotional commitment, it also brings them into the creative and innovative thinking realm of the organization.

Through the use of virtual reality technology, organizations can create new experiences to not only engage the customer, but to create virtual open spaces to connect people around the globe, to engage them in virtual collaborative environments that allow for real-time design thinking and innovation, and to share ideas not just through static visuals. Instead, they use tools and technologies that allow for the visual sharing and building of ideas that capture and expand the dynamics of the moment rather than holding them in place or keeping them in the past.

The point is that the means through which to create open spaces for design thinking are abundant. Consistent among the organizations in our research, is how they respond to the need for paying attention to, and strategically developing this attribute. We concluded that any organization, of any size can develop this particular capability. Often, the creation of open space is the change that produces change. What is vitally important to understand is that any time an organization brings together people, whether in a physical or virtual space, creating it in an intentional manner—one that lends itself to the use of design thinking—will almost always result in greater levels of new ideas and innovative solutions.

For some of you reading this book, perhaps you're already working in, or have a leadership role in, an organization through which you've experienced the energy of open spaces and realize its great value. Perhaps you've experienced a unique moment, wherein you participated in a retreat or design thinking experience in a geographic locale far from the one you typically work in or engaged with others in a historic location that evoked a deep connection to the roots of your organization or team's purpose and mission. Or, you may be looking at the attribute of open space for the first time or with a new interest in the possibilities it presents. In light of those possibilities, we thought it valuable to include a checklist of sorts that you

OPEN SPACE ELEMENTS

▶ Open community meeting areas
▶ Cultural artifacts
▶ Natural light/comfortable illumination
▶ Moderate noise levels/good acoustics
▶ Raised tables and chairs
▶ Comfortable chairs, furnishings, pillow chairs
▶ Pleasing colors
▶ Internal branding
▶ Mobile round tables
▶ Height-adjustable desks and workstations
▶ Wiring/hot desks
▶ Whiteboards, whitewalls, and flipcharts for writing and drawing on
▶ Things to write and draw with; markers of multiple colors
▶ Sticky notes of various sizes and colors
▶ Audio visual technology
▶ Prototyping materials: cardboard, tape, glue, modeling materials, magazines
▶ LEGO stuff
▶ Good climate/comfortable temperature
▶ Customers
▶ Healthy snacks and refreshments
▶ Musical instruments
▶ Toys
▶ Things to throw
▶ Espresso machines and all manner of tasty beverages

can use in creating open space or that you can apply to conduct an audit of the current design thinking space. Either way, our intention is to add to your success and help you, as the reader—in our customer experience—to get the greatest value from this book as you can.

Lastly, the attribute of open space is about the environment people will interact in and should not be confused with the idea of safe space. The creation of a safe space requires attention to how design thinking is facilitated and led, focusing on creating free expression, communication, and idea-sharing that are risk-free and as fearless as possible.

13

Whole Communication

*"The single biggest problem in communication
is the illusion that it has taken place."*
—George Bernard Shaw

Whole communication can be defined as the broader means in which human beings verbally and nonverbally communicate a message. It builds on the idea of communication: the process of sharing ideas, thoughts, and feelings with other people, and having those ideas, thoughts, and feelings understood by the people we are communicating with. Whole communication engages various forms of logical and emotional expression. From the use of data and basic visuals, to the use of painting and improv acting, whole communication allows for the spectrum of possibilities and tools to be used in telling or creating a story. Individually and collectively, they can also be creatively applied to solving problems.

The companies in our study group demonstrate an increased competency to communicate in a variety of creative ways. We were pleasantly surprised to find that these organizations are great storytellers, creators, and users of visual information, and have a willingness to experiment with new ways to communicate, interact, and brainstorm. This is particularly true when it comes to how they communicate in their use of design thinking. They appear to understand that innovation does not happen by doing surveys and writing comprehensive reports or slide decks with facts and figures. Innovation happens by contextual inquiry, discovering unarticulated needs, synthesizing, creating with empathy, and communicating solutions in methods that embrace the emotions underlining the concepts. They are able to both see the stories in the problems and challenges they undertake. They are also able to tell a new story. Through design thinking, they are able to deconstruct a story and rewrite it, and to innovate to write a new one.

One only has to look at the requirements for an MBA or engineering degree to find that curriculum guidelines emphasize written communication and quantitative research. In comparison, the practice of design thinking places emphasis on visual and verbal communication and qualitative research.

ADVENTUROUS MRI MACHINES

There's a good chance that if you haven't already undergone medical imaging, at some point in your life, you'll likely have the experience. If you have, you're already aware of what the technology, the machinery looks and feels like, as well as the room that you went into. If you haven't undergone medical imaging, go online and have a look at what the technology and setting look like, and imagine what the experience would be like. Or ask someone who has undergone an MRI to share their experience. They will likely tell you about how impersonal it is: the bland colors, and the sterile feeling and aroma of the room. Someone may tell you how noisy it was, or how claustrophobic it felt, not being able to move, lying flat on the thin shelf as they were enclosed in the MRI machine's tube, or how alone and scared they felt.

Now imagine yourself as a 6-year-old undergoing the same experience. Or, as a parent, having to walk your 5-year-old into the room for an MRI, trying to convince them to be brave enough, and knowing you won't be able to stay with them as they undergo the scan. Those who've had that experience know the level of anxiety, stress, and fear associated with it.

We heard and uncovered multiple stories of the powerful ways in which design thinking impacted lives in positive ways and contributed to making the world a better place, and benefitting the organizations that brought them into existence. Among the stories, Doug Dietz, innovation architect at GE Healthcare, tells one that stands out. As a principal designer for GE Healthcare, Doug had been designing diagnostic imaging equipment for more than 20 years. One day, he excitedly went to see a large MR scanning machine, a project that he had worked on for two years, that was just installed in a hospital.

While at the hospital where the new machine was installed, Doug watched as two parents led their 7-year-old daughter into the MR room for a scan. The child was visibly afraid, as were the parents, who, despite their fears, were trying to convince their weeping daughter to be brave. As he watched from just outside the room, the young girl froze and then broke down crying. The parents looked at each other, lost, not knowing what to say or do next.

In that moment, Doug realized that the child's actual experience of the technology that he helped to design and create resulted in an awful customer experience. The experience of the child and her parents was vastly different from that which he had just moments before, when he entered the MR suite to delight in his accomplishment of the technology he helped create. He realized the affect the large machine that "looked like a big brick with a hole in it," the dimly lit beige room, and the radioactivity warning signs had on the girl and her parents. In Doug's own words, his reaction to his discovery was that the customer experience was "awful." He felt like he had failed.

He then came to find out that because children were often so terrified by the prospect of lying alone inside the huge, noisy machine, that more than 80 percent had to be sedated prior to the procedure.

When telling his story, Doug's voice waivers, and he fights back his emotion and his tears. In response to his experience, he put together a team of experts, including staff from a local children's museum, kids, parents, and hospital staff. The children, along with other members of the team, were given crayons and asked to take on the role of designers and create adventures. Led by the children, together they designed a set of adventures that were then translated into the design of MR machines and imaging suites that brought their stories to life.[1]

The outcome was a set of adventurous experiences that children, instead of being afraid of, wanted to engage in: a Jungle Adventure that includes a patient table fashioned a after a canoe; Cozy Camp with a table that looks like a sleeping bag and with stars on the ceiling; Coral City with bubbles rotating over the ceiling and around the walls; and Pirate Island, with a plank that children walk down to get on the scanning table. The use of comforting colors, and murals and furnishings that are a part of the theme, are much more welcoming to children and invite them to use their imaginations. To touch as many of the senses as possible, the adventures even include aromatics: a sea breeze scent for Pirate Island and a piña colada aroma for Coral City.

> In design thinking, the first step of empathy is motivated by the need to understand the customer or user experience.

The innovative, design-driven solutions that Doug and his band of experts, parents, and children produced completely transformed the MR experience for children, as well as for their parents, who are the actual customers. Not to be lost in the feel-good impact of the design efforts are the more practical business outcomes—the numbers. In the hospital in which they installed the first adventure MR machines, the number of sedations went from 80 percent of patients down to a mere two children per year. Patient satisfaction increased by close to 90 percent, which in turn attracted more parents and patients. Due to the increased speed that patients now underwent scans, better scheduling led to more patients being seen, which led to increased revenue. Needless to say, the benefits achieved were extraordinary.

THE POWER OF STORYTELLING

One of the more powerful aspects of design thinking, and an element of whole communication that can be easily overlooked, is the natural relationship to, and use of, storytelling. When we look at the frameworks and models for design thinking that the organizations in our study group use—some tailored to the individual organization—the five key elements of *empathy, define, ideate, prototype*, and *test* are, in one form or another, always present.

The first of these, empathy, is the starting point. Aimed at understanding the customer experience, or story, it is the natural first step. Empathy at the outset provides for the insight into the emotional aspects of the customer experience, and that leads to the discovery of meaning, an understanding and appreciation of the importance of the human experience. The customer's experience is their story and listening with empathy requires the intention of understanding the customer's point of view. Without doing so, it becomes almost impossible to innovate a solution and create the change that truly responds to the customer's core need.

Every story has five main elements: theme, context, characters, conflict, and a resolution. With respect to a customer's story, a broad array of themes is possible. These include and are not limited to: product usability, quality, customer service, value perception, access to service, product knowledge, affordability, availability of information, engagement, responsiveness, or how the customer feels cared for.

The second element of the customer's story is context, the time and place of the customer's experience. This requires understanding the when and where (time and place) or the setting in which the customer has the experience. Next up are the characters. In most stories, there is a recognizable main character. Looking at it through the lens of design thinking, the main character is the customer. What makes main characters so interesting and useful to our stories is our ability to identify with them. Why? They have the same needs and desires that we all share as human beings.

This simple truth provides the pathways that allow people to understand the main characters' dilemma and problem they are faced with trying to resolve. If people are aware and understand themselves, they are better able to understand others. And if people have some idea as to what their emotional response is to a situation, they are more able to understand the emotion of others. One person's emotional response in a specific situation is not necessarily the same as others. This understanding allows each person to observe how, and inquire as to why, another person is responding in the manner that they are, regardless whether it is the same as or different from their own emotion and behavior.

This is how we arrive at understanding the conflicts that the main characters and other supporting characters in the story are confronted with. Once the problem is clearly defined, they can begin to find the resolution to their conflicts. In design thinking, the first step of empathy is motivated by the need to understand the customer or user experience. This requires us to focus on who the main character or characters are, and understanding their experience. Once that happens, you can move on to defining the problem that you wish to seek a solution, or set of solutions, for, thereby identifying clearly the problem that needs to solved.

Doug Dietz's story at GE Healthcare provides us with an excellent example of how storytelling becomes such a valuable asset of design thinking. As so often is our experience, Doug's first impression is that of his own experience: He was at first very happy at his accomplishment and then, upon watching the young girl and her parents, disappointed. We now recognize the girl and the parents as the key characters. Through his observation of them, Doug quickly began to empathize and began to understand the problem. By doing so, he quickly realized the emotional aspects of the conflict that the young patient had, as well as the emotional experience of the parents and their conflict over not knowing how to manage the situation.

One can easily see how exploring the context of the MR room, in relationship to the characters, led to exploring and defining the problem that needed solving. Not only did Doug's perspective shift from his design experience focused on the technology to one of empathy for the user, a key innovation question emerged: What could we imagine to create to provide a new and better experience for the patients and their parents?

Stories are a form of whole communication that connect people and allow them to experience common ground, including at the emotional level. They can be useful as a creative reminder of an organization's or group's purpose, and how individuals connect and contribute to it. They can also be helpful in changing perspective and thereby producing meaningful change.

Using whole communication, Doug and his team set out to find and design a solution. The key to doing so relied on the creation of a new story. Using the visual art form of drawing, the team created set of storyboards to respond to the emotional needs of the customer. The new story became the guide for the design of the solution, the MR adventures. The aforementioned results speak for themselves, as they do for the great outcomes resulting from the use of whole communication.

VISUAL STRENGTH

The visualization of information and storytelling of problems and solutions is paramount to design thinking success. For this to happen successfully requires whole communication, an approach to communicating across the broad span of available methods, all of which tie back to the realization of the influence and importance of human emotion. At some point, the organizations in our study group arrived at a moment of understanding that, when it comes to engaging stakeholders to embrace and contribute to the development of ideas and solving the right problems, emotion matters.

> The visualization of information and storytelling of problems and solutions are paramount to design thinking success.

Reaching this level of understanding and developing the attribute of whole communication are not all that easy. For the most part over the history of business, organizations have relied more on the use of data and logic and have struggled with the emotional content of how their people work together. The reluctance to confront and deal with emotional issues has long been one of the biggest challenges that organizations struggled with. As a result, organizations were designed to work in the world of logic, and the workforce that fed into it was prepared accordingly. This makes design thinking even that much more attractive as a means to overcome the consequences of the over reliance on data-driven approaches.

One only has to look at the requirements for an MBA or engineering degree to find that curriculum guidelines emphasize written communication and qualitative research. In comparison, one only has to look at the practice of design thinking to find an emphasis on visual and verbal communication and quantitative research. Emotion-based, informative, and interactive forms of communication have the power to multiply engagement, to tell a story with emotion in order to get multiple stakeholders to engage, embrace, and contribute to the development of solving the right problems. Design thinking connects the left side of the brain (the source of the analytic and logical reasoning functions) with the right side (the source of creativity, imagination, and intuitive thinking). There is recognition that within all forms of data, there is a story. The result is a more holistic approach to exploring and solving problems, and innovating.

> Design thinking connects the left side of the brain (the source of the analytic and logical reasoning functions) with the right side (the source of creativity, imagination, and intuitive thinking).

To better understand the relevance of whole communication as an attribute of innovative organizations requires us to connect to how we communicate emotion in the ways that go beyond the immediate verbal and nonverbal means, and to recognize that we engage in the various forms of art and apply them to how we innovate. In business, our innovation is manifested through how we create products and services, and the experiences that respond to the emotional needs of customers.

One of the more powerful qualities of design thinking is that it can be used to engage people in the use of a variety of art forms and ways in which to both communicate and create new ideas. Furthermore, it intensifies the relationship between the emotional aspects that drive creativity with the logical approaches of data and our pursuit of knowledge. All too often the two are seen as separate. In design thinking and the application of whole communication, we experience the intimate relationship of the two and how, in fact, truly interdependent they are.

14

Aligned Leadership

> "*True leaders don't create followers.*
> *They create more leaders.*"
> —Unknown

When we first set out on this research project, we were curious as to the level of support for design thinking that leaders in the organizations in our study group demonstrated. That is, how aligned is their commitment and what strategies were they using to align leadership? We were also curious as to how effective leaders had to be at empowering others in the organization, especially other leaders, to use design thinking throughout their organizations. From our point of view, the use of design thinking would likely require leaders to "let go," thereby allowing others to create strategies, make decisions, and play a more integral role in how the organization functions.

We were also curious whether there was any one style of leadership that lends itself better to design thinking than others and to what degree the styles of leaders create differences in how design thinking is supported throughout an organization. We were also interested in what specific leadership behaviors are essential to the success of leaders in design thinking organizations.

Our curiosity in all three areas produced important insights. What we learned about commitment and support of design thinking is not more important than the insights we gained about style, nor is style more important than the behaviors attributed to leadership success. We'll leave the rankings of importance to you, allowing you to explore and decide, from your own perspective, what you find to be most valuable. We can suggest with a sense of certainty that effectively using design thinking to leverage the collective imagination that resides within any organization requires elements of all three.

The key outcomes:

- The level of commitment and support shown by leaders for the use and integration of design thinking, including the development of leaders in their organizations, and involving and empowering other design thinking experts, is *the* key factor to success.
- The more successful leaders effectively role-model and reinforce the behaviors associated with design thinking, thereby gaining a reputation as being open and receptive to change, the greater their influence.
- Although the style of leadership can vary and is unique to the individual, the more aligned the style or type of leadership is to the culture, the more effective the leader.

ON THE MATTER OF COMMITMENT

In a 1973 lecture at the University of Pennsylvania, Thomas Watson Jr., then IBM's chief executive, declared, "Good design is good business."[1] This statement has become a mantra for designers all around the world. Some say the phrase was written by famous graphic designer Paul Rand, who designed the IBM logo, and was working with and helping Watson Jr. understand the power and value of design. Regardless of who gets final credit, at IBM, the idea stuck.

A succession of CEOs at IBM, starting with Watson, have a long history working with some of the world's best designers of their times. The story starts in the 1950s, when IBM was inspired by, or jealous of, the design, beauty, and usability of Olivetti typewriters. At the time, the Italian company was a key IBM competitor. This inspired IBM to get serious about design in order to compete on a global scale. (It's too bad the likes of GM, Ford, Chrysler, and many other large corporations didn't catch the same inspiration from great Italian design back then.)

Since then IBM has commissioned very long retained engagements with design icons including Paul Rand, Eliot Noyes, Ray and Charles Eames, Isamu Noguchi, and Richard Sapper, among others. This has influenced IBM's philosophy of design over decades and helped enable them to be a design leader. And today, this same inspiration and commitment, one could say, is being engaged with their company-wide commitment to design thinking. "We live in the shadow of what Eliot Noyes and the Eames's, Rand and Saarinen have done," says Keith Yamashita, the IBM Charles and Ray Eames Brand Fellow. "It's the same mission. It's just different people."

Today, IBM is one of the most committed companies to design thinking on the planet, a result of its consistently aligned leadership. From Watson Jr., to Lou Gerstner, to today's Ginni Rometty, CEO after CEO has supported good design, assuring its successful cascading and growth throughout the organization. The IBM Design Thinking initiative started in 2013, when the company became determined to create a sustainable culture of design, at a very large scale. The engine that powers this transformation is IBM Design Thinking. They've created a framework for applying design thinking at the speed and scale demanded by an enterprise as dynamic as IBM. The ultimate goal is to align with the corporate goals of IBM: "To change the way IBM approaches problems and solutions to improve the lives of the people we serve." In 2015, in a small workshop in Dublin, Ireland, a handful of designers and design leaders gathered and spent a few days using design thinking to review how it was being used at IBM. One of the outcomes was the simple phrase "IBM Design Thinking for All."

Now well into the program, IBM Design Thinking has touched more than 50,000 employees with training, one the largest and most aggressive design thinking initiatives we researched. Currently, Doug Powell, a distinguished designer with IBM, is leading the design thinking initiative.

Currently, Doug Powell, a distinguished designer with IBM, is leading the design thinking initiative. IBM Design is so engrained, and so influential, it acts as a separate business unit. As Doug says, the mission of IBM Design is to create a sustainable culture for design and design thinking. There is an explicit cultural change component to this mission. The objective is not to just hire more designers and not to do design thinking for the sake of it. It's about how the organization uses design thinking to solve problems.

To scale design and design thinking across organization they established three strategies: people, places, and practices.

People: They had to significantly increase human resources, and improve the ratio of designers to employees. Since 2012 they have had a new increase of 1,500 designers. Today, IBM may well be the world's largest employer of product and UX designers.

Places: As part of the strategy, the company built a centralized design studio in Austin, Texas. At 120,000 square feet, it acts as a home base for 350 designers. Around the globe today, IBM has 36 different design studios.

Practices: The establishment of IBM Design (also referred to as D Framework), the company's program being used to integrate design thinking throughout the organization.

Unlike the roots of the design leadership at IBM in the past decades, which was essentially emerged from brand and industrial design services for hardware and communication design, the corporate design group today has its roots in software and UX product design, which helps better enable user experience and human-centered design strategies. This creates a very significant contribution to the company and more meaningful experiences for their customers.

As the IBM website states, "We believe human experiences drive business."[2]

3M: MOVING TOWARD COLLABORATIVE CREATIVITY

It's true: 3M still has the 15-percent rule for innovation. It is deeply embedded in its culture and is encouraged through the commitment of its leadership. Over time, this was considered such a powerful strategy that other companies in search of greater innovation, including Google and Intuit, followed suit. But there is more: One aspect of its evolution at 3M is the increased use of design thinking in making use of this unstructured, creative time.[3]

Today, Eric Quint is the chief design officer at 3M. He joined the company in 2013, as their first company-wide CDO. He serves on the executive leadership team, and his charter is to build and lead the design function as a vital competitive platform across the enterprise. As you may suspect, Eric is using design thinking to accomplish this objective. He told us that 3M is committed to adding design successfully to its portfolio, recognizing that design enriches innovation and differentiation through brand experience. Eric states that adding design to a global company will have a transformational impact on the culture and DNA of the company, and that, in order to do so, there must be an alignment between executive leadership and the chief design officer and their organization.

At 3M, design thinking is seen as a tool for this transformation, as well as for collaboration. "It is a collaborative creation tool. And, it's about doing things differently. Integrating design is also about building trust and stimulating inclusion, and that's where design thinking comes into play."[4] When we asked Eric how aligned leadership is at the executive level, he told us that design thinking is on the senior executive agenda and includes the head of HR.

Three years ago, they began the initiative by using design thinking to envision and create their upcoming design thinking program. Eric and his team first did contextual research and benchmarked with other successful companies at scaling design thinking. They set a strategy in place, prototyped training, ran pilot projects with internal users, iterated, and then built a suite of custom training assets. After more pilots and refinements, they are preparing this year to roll out a full program. The use of design thinking is very much in alignment with the historical strategy of employee innovation at 3M. Eric predicts that design and design thinking will become part of the DNA of 3M. He adds that it has the power to change the way people think, act, and collaborate to impact all processes and phases of the business. Eric suggests, "A design leader must be empathetic, driven by curiosity to observe people beyond mere dialog. Through empathy, design leaders will better understand the needs of customers to support relevant innovations, drive great brand experiences, demonstrate great design leadership to their teams, and enable cross-functional collaboration."

Further, Eric points out:

Creativity is not solely owned by the design function, it ranges across all functions. Design thinking is a great tool for collaboration as it is a multidisciplinary, problem-solving approach using creativity and insights to solve complex challenges. Anybody can participate in a design thinking approach, but that doesn't make everybody a designer. Design thinking is a great way to enable creative collaboration and co-creation across disciplines; it demonstrates the added value of designers and helps distinguish between design thinking as a creative problem-solving approach from design as an act of art craftsmanship.

Eric is driving transformation in the company by using design and design thinking to change the company over the next period. He says adding a chief design officer to a global company has a significant impact on the company. Eric's approach is in line with a favorite quote from John Maeda, American designer and technologist, whose work explores the area where business, design, and technology merge: "Inclusiveness isn't about you, it's about making space for others to be themselves." What is Eric's challenge to the world? "What country will be the first to have a Chief Design Officer?" Great question.

These lessons represent a powerful study in leadership alignment and commitment and are an example of what we discovered in many of the companies in our study: the more direct and simple the strategy—like IBM's "people, places, practice" approach—the greater the likelihood of success. At its best, design thinking provides for simple and powerful solutions to even the most difficult and complex of problems. The simple approaches that IBM and 3M take to their design thinking strategies can work for any size organization. Though the size and scope may vary, the simple approaches that the organizations in our study group use will work anywhere.

ROLE-MODELING ALIGNMENT

While committing to the idea that design thinking is important to culture, and that scaling it requires alignment to that intention, we found that how leaders role-model is a critical factor. This is a key ingredient to how well leaders support design and the use of design thinking through their organizations, as well as how they empower others to set and influence strategy, and make decisions. The further we explored how innovative organizations are led, the more we discovered that many of the CEOs are either leading a design-driven organization or are strategically pursuing the goal of transforming their company into one, and that the commitment they demonstrate from their own involvement and learning, and active role in the use of design thinking, plays an integral role in their success.

Jeff Immelt's commitment to moving GE's headquarters to Boston, Massachusetts, and Rice's mandate for greater collaboration across the company, including embracing the influence of the rising creative class, is a great example. When Craig Meller, CEO at AMP, first experienced design thinking training and the impact it was having on his employees, he had his old mahogany boardroom turned into a light and bright creative workspace, and began holding his executive meetings surrounded by whiteboards instead of PowerPoint projectors and extension cords. As mentioned in

Chapter 12, this quickly caught on. In a about a year, every floor of the company's 25-floor headquarters had innovation labs. Similar spaces for creative collaboration at Autodesk, Visa, 3M, SAP, Intuit, and others are evidence of the ability of the leadership to understand the powerful influence that design thinking brings to their companies. Commitment matters. This includes not just speaking the language of design and innovation. It includes direct involvement in the use of design thinking, the role-modeling of design thinking behaviors, and the strategic support of design thinking in the organizations they lead, or a leader in.

What does that ideal leader look like? It would be nice to present a profile of a personality and leadership type, or a predictable definition of what particular style works best, but that's not the case. Whether someone is an outgoing leader and communicator, a quiet engineer, an A-type driver of performance and outcomes, a T-shaped innovator, a servant leader that thrives on being liked and admired, or a top-down planner and strategist, regardless of style or role, the consistent set of factors that make for their success are more related to the influence they get through acting in alignment to the company's culture and purpose. The belief and commitment they show through their leadership and strategic support of, and participation in, design thinking and the innovation it contributes to their companies also matters. The influence these leaders gain from demonstrating their alignment and commitment allows the people in their companies to see value in the process of design thinking, engage in it, and advocate its use. It also gives them

What's truly powerful is that the more a leader engages in design thinking, the more they begin to integrate the behaviors associated with design thinking into their leadership behavior. They become better listeners, better inquirers, and more collaborative in how they coach and solve problems with others. In doing so, they show greater levels of empathy, resulting in a better understanding of how to more effectively engage and motivate employees.

the ability to produce change, innovate new ideas, and as we pointed out in the opening chapter of this book, to perform at greater levels.

Such leaders further that influence and the alignment of the culture by also expecting the other leaders in the organization to follow suit. They are the primary catalysts for aligned leadership at the other levels of the organization and have a significant influence on how teams function and behave. They invest in internal and external resources to build their own competencies, as well as others. They engage and take part in developing structures and processes to support collaboration and involvement with designers throughout the company, and envisioning new process solutions. One of the keys to these efforts and others is the effect it has on how leaders in their organizations perceive their relationship to change.

One of the greatest investments that highly innovative organizations make is in the development and alignment of their leaders. This is an aspect of alignment from the top. As Peter Chrisp, CEO of NZTE, explained to us, he believes that alignment has played a big role in NZTE's identity as an innovative organization. He also sees the role of alignment to the clear strategic direction in how it is applied: "It underlines the power of having a framework for alignment and staying focused on the customer. The entire team needs to be wrapped around the customer. True alignment is a fundamental truth." Reaching this kind of alignment doesn't happen without a focus on the alignment of leadership behavior.

Peter also points out the need for leadership to be open to the innovative disruption that design thinking can deliver. Being able to make use of that level of innovation requires leaders to be better listeners and fearlessly explore possibilities. According to Peter, one of the most important aspects of aligned leadership is a willingness to be open. He says, "Open to listening to our customers: openness to other employees; open to new ideas; open to challenging our differences; open to failure; open to taking on the most difficult of challenges. Most importantly, open to change."

The alignment and role-modeling by leaders in design thinking cultures are key to how well an organization's employees feel empowered to engage in the behaviors that support the successful use of design thinking. This requires leaders to learn the value of design thinking and its powerful influence in the development of a culture of innovation. Leaders need to embody the values and beliefs of that culture and to commit to the development of aligned leaders throughout the organization. As Peter Chrisp so wisely observed, "Now that we've designed our culture, we've got to do the hard work of making sure we are all aligned in the design of our leadership...and be clear about our behaviors as leaders."

Leaders must have the ability to understand the key characteristics and traits of culture, and recognize what leadership behavior is aligned and what behavior is not. And if they choose to use behaviors that are inconsistent with the expectations set by the culture, they are best advised to clearly articulate the reasoning behind their choices and actions. If they don't, they run the risk of losing the trust of others.

STYLE MATTERS

With respect to our curiosity regarding styles of leadership, it does have a direct impact on a leader's success. It just may not be in the manner that one would readily expect. When we talk about leadership, along with the long list of qualities that we see as being consistent to great leadership—vision, determination, forthrightness, accountability, work ethic, compassion, confidence, and more—we typically turn to talking about leadership as a style or type, and then venture into trying to figure out what the best style or approach is. Inevitably, that takes us to the conversation of whether the leader is the right one for the time and place, or if they are right as the main character that fits the context they find themselves in.

We found that leadership styles can vary, but one of the foundational elements to success is that the individual's leadership style is aligned with the culture of the organization.[5] If the style of leadership is at odds with the culture, regardless of how well intentioned the leader is, they will have a difficult time succeeding. Success requires leaders to gain intimate knowledge of the culture and choose behaviors that allow them to integrate and align to what is expected by the culture. The vast majority of the CEOs in our study did the same. Having intimate knowledge of the culture is one of the reasons that the succession of leaders is often perceived as an important step in the sustainability and growth of an organization. Our study also demonstrates it to be an important aspect of how several of the organizations have maintained their ability to innovate organically over time.

In our look at defining what the ideal leadership is that is in alignment to, and best supports design thinking, we identified a set of attributes that are worthwhile sharing. If anything, it may serve as a guide for the assessment of your own leadership.

One of the most important aspects of aligned leadership is a willingness to be open.

The Attributes of Design Thinking Leaders:

▶ Uses empathy to understand the experiences of others.

▶ Focuses on creating a benefit for the customer.

▶ Listens with mutual respect and fearless exploration to understand others.

▶ Openly expresses their ideas and what they think, see, and feel.

▶ Pursues knowledge by being curious, inquiring, and asking questions.

▶ Demonstrates the ability to be vulnerable, including accepting of their mistakes and incompetence.

▶ Coaches others, rather than sharing viewpoint and competing with others.

▶ Relies on the knowledge and insight of others, and not acting as the lone genius.

▶ Strives for self-knowledge and uses the personal power of choice.

▶ Uses curious confrontation to effectively manage disagreement and conflict.

▶ Aligns their personal purpose in contribution to the organization's mission.

There are additional attributes that you can add to the list and that you can observe in others, as well as yourself. The study of leadership is one of the broadest examples of our quest to better understand humankind's journey. In this chapter, we are only touching on one small aspect of the extraordinary body of work on the subject. That said, we hope we've captured it in a manner that is useful to you.

15

Purpose

"Passion is caring deeply about something. Purpose is doing something about what you deeply care about."
— Edgar Papke

As we have explored throughout this book, innovation is a never-ending pursuit of business. Why? It's human nature. This simple understanding will help to remind you of the greatest value of design thinking. It provides a process for the open exploration of possibility, a method for innovating that allows us to fully engage one another in the creation of a shared future. Innovation is art. Innovation is business. Business is humankind's most advanced form of art and the most innovative expression of the collective imagination.

The organizations in our study demonstrate a sense of purpose in bringing something of value to the world. They show the ability to successfully integrate two key aspects of innovative success: the external focus on the customer, and the internal focus on their cultures and how they do things. A commonsense approach to the tension that exists in the relationship between the two tells us that this is an obvious requirement to success. Much like individual human beings do, organizations need to be aware of who they are in relationship to the world they live in.

The simple truth is that, for any organization to be innovative requires it to have a shared set of ideals as to its purpose for existence. Why? If members are in alignment with an organization's purpose for existence, they will be more engaged and more motivated in how they think and act. Customers and their audience at large are connected, living in a world that continues to rapidly change and in which people are participants and contributors to the ongoing change. They want to know more and be a part of it. And if they're going to be taking part in it, they want to know more about why and how things are happening. They want to know the purpose behind it. They want to engage to contribute more and feel like the purpose behind a product or service matters to them. Whether it's logical or purely intuitive, it comes back to the core.

One of the greatest values of design thinking is that it provides a process for the open exploration of possibility, a method for innovating that allows us to fully engage one another in the creation of a shared future.

20 YEARS AGO...

In 1994, in the book *Built to Last*, Jim Collins and Jerry Porras wrote about the powerful purpose of Johnson & Johnson (J&J).[1] At that time, a new attention was brought to the power of an organization's purpose, and J&J was at the center of that attention. Here we are more than 20 years later, and though the world has undergone significant change, the J&J mission remains the same: "To help people live longer, happier and healthier lives."[2] What has changed about the company is how it goes about delivering to its purpose. Ernesto Quinteros, J&J's chief design officer, shared with us:

> Our Credo, written in 1943, directly aligns with the principles of design thinking. At Johnson & Johnson, we have made

it our mission to help people live longer, healthier and happier lives, which is why we put individuals at the core of everything we do. Our design thinking initiatives are inspired by Our Credo and our passion to understand and create transformational solutions for the entire ecosystem of care.

This powerful statement tying design thinking to J&J's mission reinforces the idea that when innovation is at its best, it is an expression of human need and desire, and evokes a sense of human value. Because design has been recognized as a people-centered discipline, it is often used as a connector. According to Ernesto:

Design is getting involved in multiple initiatives across Johnson & Johnson. For example, we're co-leading efforts to ensure that our Credo and purpose give us a stronger rallying cry for the next generation. We are a large, complex, diversified organization that has grown organically, and through numerous acquisitions for over 130 years, and it is critical that we are all marching towards the same purpose. Design can play a key translation role in making that purpose more tangible and influencing the behavior of our 130,000 employees. We are partnering closely with HR to help integrate this purpose statement into initiatives focused on the overall employee experience.

The approach to design at J&J is defined as Care-Centered Design. It's people-centered because the word *care* implies deep empathy, a very human quality. "We wanted to differentiate our approach and create a strong and authentic connection to Our Credo and mission to help people live longer, happier and healthier lives."

The focus is on two goals:

1. To deliver on innovation and brand experience projects across three sectors (Consumer, Pharmaceuticals, and Medical Devices) of a $71B enterprise.
2. To embed design thinking methods into the organization. This takes the form of training—typically delivered in a

workshop format—that uses design thinking to address key business challenges.

Design thinking is endorsed across the entire organization, including support and sponsorship from C-suite executives. Because design is driving innovation across the enterprise and is a key part of the approach to innovation, it is directly embedded in each sector of J&J. The enterprise-wide chief design officer role was created in 2014 to signify the commitment and reach of design.

Here are some examples of the success of design thinking in delivering solutions: From a service perspective, Johnson & Johnson Design developed a blueprint for Alzheimer's patients and their families, as well as creating website recommendations specific to patient education. In regard to the design thinking of experiences, the design team has partnered with IBM and Johnson & Johnson's Health and Wellness Solutions team on Health Partner, a digital suite of tools that helps patients throughout the surgical decision and recovery process, and will connect them to their care provider. It's a wonderful example of how J&J is working with its partners and patients to develop new, design-inspired, behavioral science-based, tech-driven solutions for every individual. They are also applying design thinking to deal with open-ended problems, which encourage multiple paths to multiple solutions (divergence), rather than limit thinking (convergence). Oftentimes the journey when dealing with open-ended problems yields innovative and fresh ideas for future pursuit.

According to Ernesto, the design organization already has a collaborative culture, but design thinking has facilitated collaborations across functional partner teams that ordinarily would not occur. Embracing divergence, experimentation, and different points of view enriches collaborations that may have previously followed more conventional methods. "With support from our leadership, we continue to evolve with openness to more and radically different propositions, including overt messages about failing fast, being bold and experimenting outside one's comfort zone." So far, J&J has trained 700 people in design thinking and the plan is train another 20,000 people in 2018.

GETTING TO #1

In 2006, Chef Daniel Humm and restaurateur Will Guidara partnered to open a restaurant in New York City, a brasserie, with an ambition to turn it into one of the great restaurants of the world. Early on, they received a small and not very noteworthy review from the *New York Observer*. Although it wasn't the best of reviews (nor the worst), something that the reviewer wrote about Humm and Guidara's restaurant stuck. The reviewer commented that the restaurant was good, but it was missing something. The restaurant "[n]eeded a bit more Miles Davis." From Chef Daniel and Will's perspective, that came to be an important moment in their collaboration, creating a sense of clarity to their pursuit and purpose. They decided to channel the attributes of the great jazz musician Miles Davis, known as a genius at improvisation and collaboration, into their restaurant.

In recognition of their passionate commitment to their craft, they adopted a set of characteristics that capture the spirit of Miles. The descriptive traits also convey the passion of their promise to deliver to patrons through the experience of their restaurant:

- Cool.
- Endless reinvention.
- Forward-moving.
- Fresh.
- Collaborative.

- Spontaneous.
- Vibrant.
- Adventurous.
- Light.
- Innovative.

Over time they set out to be "the most delicious and gracious restaurant in the world." Chef Daniel reflects, "At that moment I realized we had all of these amazing creative chefs and cooks on our staff. I realized we needed more collaboration. The food had to become more personal."

In 2010, Eleven Madison Park (EMP), the restaurant with plenty of "Miles" achieved a ranking of #50 on the list of the best restaurants in the world. In April 2017, it was honored with the #1 spot, the world's best restaurant, according to World's 50 Best Restaurants, the most authoritative and definitive restaurant ranking in the world. Getting on the list has, by most estimations, become a higher prize than earning three Michelin stars, an accomplishment EMP and many of the selected restaurants have achieved. It is only the second American restaurant in history to be named the world's #1. (The other is Thomas Keller's the French Laundry, in Napa Valley, California, in 2003 and 2004.)

What is truly amazing is that, whereas most restaurants don't change their menu very often once they get the coveted three Michelin stars, EMP changes its menu four times a year, to coincide with the changing seasons. It takes about three months to develop a new menu for the upcoming season, and unique themes, so they are in a continuous innovation mode. At the core of their passion and purpose, Chef Daniel told us that he and Will set out to create an expression of art, a restaurant that like its owners, continues to change and grow. As Chef Daniel shared with us, "You have to be true to yourself. You have to be creative to change and grow as you do." This passion for seeing food as art and sense of purpose is not lost on the Eleven Madison Park's staff—nor is it lost on its customers.

According to Will, the culture of EMP is an extremely collaborative one. They believe that including the talented staff is essential to the success of the restaurant. This, too, is quite amazing, because most of the worlds three-star Michelin restaurants are so-called "chef-driven." EMP is different. They hold all-employee meetings and annual all-hands strategic planning retreats, and have learned how to capture the creative talent of their employees. Will explained that there are three key reasons for the strategic planning meetings. One is to tap into all of that brainpower and creativity. The second is to motivate people, to help them succeed, because they have part in the ideation and creativity, and shared commitment to be more successfully implemented. The third is that the more intentional they made the creative process, the better it became, and they've learned to leverage it expertly. Will says, "We believe that you can make creativity happen. You just need to set the conditions and then make it happen."

The culture of collaboration at EMP is built on a foundation of trust between the dining room and the kitchen. One of the keys at EMP is that Will and Chef Daniel are equal partners in the business, meaning that the dining room and the kitchen have the same amounts of influence (hence it not being a chef-run restaurant). They don't use the traditional "front of the house" and "back of the house" nomenclature; it's just the dining room and the kitchen, working together. After all, it takes both halves to create the ultimate dining experiences. Being equal means that Chef Daniel and Will always have to lead by example.

The equality between dining room and kitchen also means that the food they turn out and the service they provide are extremely collaborative. That said, there has to be in their own design language, too: The service needs to feel like Will, and the food needs to feel like Chef Daniel. The two collaborate very effectively and innovation is leveraged through the set of trusting relationships. Will and Chef Daniel agree that they have learned that this well integrated relationship is key to the success of their culture. They are the role models for how collaboration happens and how it feeds into the restaurant's purpose.

Both Will and Chef Daniel, and their staff, are as passionate as they are purpose-driven. As Chef Daniel shared with us, after a 23-year search, he finally created a dish that he believes he found his true self in. From that emerged a new language—a common language that is applied to the customer experience and that is found in everything they do. Chef Daniel explained it as "four fundamentals that are equally represented." He says:

> One, it has to be delicious, in an instant, not leaving someone to have to think about it. Two, it has to be aesthetic, to feel organic, minimal, and of effortless beauty, as if a leaf on a plate looks like it fell from the sky. Third, it has to have a high degree of creativity. It has to be something new and deliver an element of surprise, for example, perhaps an innovative new technique, or flavor combination, or two plants that grew up together. Four, it has to have intention, a purpose. It has to have a story and reason for being, like a friendship, an experience. If we can feel it, we can create it.

After a pause, Chef Daniel continued, "It's liberating to know how to speak. I get inspiration through music and art. Art is the inspiration for the work and the learning drives you. As Miles said, 'To keep creating, you have to be about change.'"

Chef Daniel and Will consider Eleven Madison Park to be "[a] single point of view restaurant." It's comprised of 150 individuals, and there is an integration of incredible creativity and collaboration, coupled with a relentless final pass on every single detail, and absolute massive micromanagement for perfection.

And having achieved the recognition as being the world's best restaurant, without calling their work design thinking, they demonstrate using many of the 10 attributes we've reviewed, including embracing the pull factor, solving the right problems, culture awareness, curious confrontation, co-creation, whole communication, aligned leadership, and purpose. But what holds all of it together is that it is supported by a joint passion to make it perfect—their simple, humble brand promise: "Make it nice."

THE PROMISE OF PURPOSE

To be purpose-driven is to hold a promise. Whether it's a large, well-established global company, or a highly innovative restaurant that reaches its goal to become the best in the world, what evokes the emotion that leverages the collective imagination is its purpose—the why it exists. One element that all the companies in our study group share is a clearly defined purpose. Some may call it a mission. When it comes to design thinking, it becomes the true intention that the resulting innovations are aimed at delivering to. It is the key to great strategic thinking, as it is the micromanagement of details in the delivery of a product or service.

Today, more than ever, this is a part of a broader and more engaged consumer ecosystem in which customers are no longer bystanders in the creative process. The fundamental rules have changed and an organization's purpose is the promise, the commitment it makes. And not only do consumers want assurance that purpose and the promise will be met, they want to be involved. They take not only the role of content and product users, but that of content creators who are engaged in the innovation process. They want involvement in the creation of what they buy.

Furthermore, they want to know the intention of the purpose of the product or service. The innovation of technology has afforded consumers with a new transparency and insight that directly reflect their attitudes and the discovery of a new sense of awareness as to who they are, why they are buying what they buy, and how they do it. There is a new generation of consumers creating a big shift. Recent studies indicate that more than seven out of 10 younger consumers want to be engaged in the creation of the products and services they are shopping for. More than seven out of 10 are more willing to pay for products and services that are seen in a positive social and environmental light.[3]

The message is a powerful one. Clearly articulating purpose is no longer a matter of influencing only the people within an organization or as a general marketing and advertising tool. It is more and more becoming an element of engagement and innovation with a broader set of participants that are savvier and more interested, and that want to be more involved. For that reason, not only does the purpose of an organization have to be emotionally compelling, it also needs to offer specificity, accessibility, powerful imagery, social benefit, environmental responsibility, strategic clarity, and continuity. Although the organizations in our study group show a purpose to their existence, they will also need to leverage those further. A good way of getting there is through the use of design thinking.

Looking Forward: Future Possibilities

"Even if you're on the right track, you'll
get run over if you just sit there."
—Will Rogers

As futurist James "Jim" Allen Dator, director of the Hawaii Research Center for Futures Studies, suggests, we cannot predict the future, but we can predict future alternatives, and we can strive for our desired future alternative. Part of that future is the emergence of design thinking as a business megatrend. As the use of design thinking continues to expand, it is difficult to argue that it will not find its way to being applied, in some shape or form, throughout the organizations of the world. To not leverage this idea would be to try to reverse the power of innovation. This, as we know, is impossible.

The future is brighter than it has ever been. Why? As demonstrated by the 21 cases in our research, design thinking methods really work. As a result, we have the ability to actually design new cultures of innovation. And because the methods of design thinking provide for tangible results, they can be embedded in organizations and have a long reach into the future. As we've already come to recognize, great innovation will stem from all people and in different creative ways: doing design thinking, being creative, collaborating, and prototyping—all leading to the solving of the right problems. Furthermore, as the case studies demonstrate, design thinking helps create relationships, even building cultures of innovation, and informs us how to develop, nurture, and more effectively lead them. This builds to the triple bottom line of any organization and society as a whole: economic value, social value, and environmental value. We believe design thinking is a megatrend; it is a most significant emerging transformational business practice, and will fuel the innovation of many smart organizations well into the foreseeable future.

> The Millennial generation, plus Generation X and Generation Z, are key ingredients in the evolution of organizations and the movement toward design thinking cultures.

The use and application of design thinking in organizations appears to be as infinite as our collective imagination can take us. As we've argued, throughout history, humankind has thrived on innovation. The future will not be different, and we will achieve better results with better methods. Therefore, the quest to build a culture of innovation will be paramount for every organization of the future. This is not exclusive to business. We believe it to be relevant to organizations and communities of all types and sizes, from profit and non-profit organizations, to public sectors, and to society on a larger scale.

We look into the future with an optimistic view of the ramifications of this body of work and possibilities for the future at the personal, organizational, and societal levels. Having the ability and methods to design innovative cultures allows us to explore potential organization models of the future that we have not yet uncovered, and probe into how they may affect the broader spectrum of social and

Ten reasons why we believe design thinking will last:

1 Design thinking is occupation independent.

2 It works.

3 It links to our basic needs as humans.

4 It helps fill some big gaps in education.

5 It helps solve any kind of problem.

6 It works great with many other business processes, like Agile, Lean, and waterfall.

7 It works great for customer experience and digital transformation.

8 The results can be measured.

9 It can be applied company-wide.

10 It's pretty cheap to do, and can save lots of money too.

global creativity, collaboration, and innovation. We see design thinking organizations as a desired alternative future.

The Millennial generation, plus Generation X and Generation Z, are key ingredients in the evolution of organizations and the movement toward design thinking cultures. As history's largest generation, Millennials are poised for greater levels of change than every other generation before it. It is a generation whose members are seeking more engagement and authenticity, involvement, and transparency. They are not just knocking at the door of business and institutional leadership with an expectation for more, they have already walked through the door and are a significant part of the business megatrend that relies on the attributes of design thinking organizations. They want more—and that's a good thing.

The organizations of the future will continue to be influenced by humankind's capability to create and innovate, and continue to better leverage the collective imagination. And they will continue to, with ever-increasing speed, confront and solve problems. They will shift from role to role, and organizations will need the means to deliver the required participation and engagement. And as people continue to move from one organization to another, and act as free agents and contractors, design thinking skills will offer a set of increasingly valuable, transferable, and occupation-independent skills. Open-minded people are craving knowledge and skills in design thinking. The convergence of the global digital economy, the desire for participation, and the emergence of the design thinking megatrend provides the ideal context for innovation at levels not yet seen.

On the other hand, it is also possible that design thinking could fade away. It could simply become status quo, an embedded method of problem-solving, and not need a separate designation anymore. And as we've seen in cases at Yahoo, Tata, and Honeywell, it can end when the executive sponsor leaves the company. It can and does fail, in certain circumstances.

Seven reasons why design thinking could fade away:

1. It's not part of STEM education, and education is stuck anyhow.

2. Little accreditation, few, if any, degrees in design thinking.

3. It's hard to measure empathy, collaboration, curiosity, change.

4. It can be hard to do; it takes time and effort.

5. It takes executive support to build out large employee training programs.

6. It challenges people and status quo; it rocks the boat.

7. It is still in prototype stage.

Our prediction is that the failure option is not likely. Are we stepping out on a limb? Not really. Our prediction is based on user collaboration and contextual inquiry. We doubt that Autodesk would train 1,000 employees; Deutche Telekom 8,000; GE Healthcare 6,000; IBM 50,000; Intuit 10,000; Kaiser 15,000; Marriott 5,000; SAP 20,000; Philips 5,000; and Visa 10 percent of their workforce on a whim. Nope. We see the winds of a megatrend emerging.

CLOSING THE EDUCATION GAP

One of the greatest benefits that design thinking can deliver, and one of its greatest challenges, is in the realm of education. Education can also deliver great benefits to design thinking. In exploring the first of these two opportunities, there is little doubt of the role design thinking can play in creating better education. As Sir Ken Robinson and others have argued, education is all too often a system based on time and performance, linearity and conformity, batching people in a mechanical process. Meanwhile, human flourishing is based on passion, and what excites humankind's spirit and creative energy. According to these critics, today's approaches to education don't feed the human spirit and passion. They argue that human learning is an organic, not mechanical, process. According to Robinson, it's creating a movement in which people can flourish. We agree with this point of view and believe that business needs to have the same response.

As people continue to move from one organization to another, and act as free agents and contractors, design thinking skills will offer a set of increasingly valuable, transferable and occupation-independent skills.

As human beings, design thinking creates a powerful link to our basic needs and desires, and makes it ideal as a path to the development of the skills and knowledge necessary to engage in the creativity and innovation required to succeed in the future. And whereas training in organizations helps fill some gaps in education, we have already arrived at the time when we realize it's not enough. Currently, despite the emergence of some design thinking curriculum, there is not enough formal education in design thinking available, and few formal degree programs are being offered. The d.school at Stanford is a highly acclaimed program, but it is not a degreed program, and it's essentially not open to the general public (excluding a very costly executive workshop program).

This is where education needs to deliver greater benefit to the design thinking movement. As further indication of the design thinking megatrend is an underlying trend in education, a review of the top business schools reveals that nearly all of them have student-led design and innovation clubs.

Certainly, one reason that design thinking isn't integrated in formal education is because it's hard to measure the learning of such activities as empathy, collaboration, curiosity, and change. For some, they can be a hard set of skills to master. That being said, when it comes to higher education, it's generally more about keeping the status quo. As much as design thinking can challenge the cultures of organizations and their leaders, the same should be said of education.

Therefore, we propose an approach to the design of curriculums and programs that takes into consideration the wide variety of possibilities in integrating education's left and right brains, a means through which design thinking can benefit education. As Albert Einstein is quoted as saying, "The most beautiful experience we can have is the mysterious. It is the fundamental emotion that stands at the cradle of true art and true science."

THE FUTURE OF DESIGN THINKING

In a previous chapter, we introduced the idea of the Fifth Order of Design: awareness. We believe this coupled with design thinking may be the answer to the long quest by HR leaders: to develop learning organizations. Design thinking itself is a learning process. By sharing this new idea, we're suggesting that to fully engage in the previous four orders of design requires people to be aware of and continuously integrate consideration of the human needs and desires that motivate our behavior. This idea is particularly noteworthy in relationship to the Fourth Order, which brings forward the design of systems, and begins to touch on social systems and the cultures of organizations. Though an awareness of human motivation is helpful and valuable in the first three orders of design, consideration of the same human motivations that manifest in the collective imagination is critical to systems design. Without the integration of the awareness of human motivation, systems cannot be designed to be flexible and agile, nor will they be able to reflect the changes resulting from humankind's ability to innovate such systems.

The true power of design thinking is that it engages the collective imagination and offers the ability to explore the underlying motivation that leads to human innovation; and that products, services, and systems can be intentionally designed to offer the insight necessary to allow their users to gain that awareness; and that we can actually design desired cultures of innovation. But when it comes to human awareness, there is never a final state. As the result of increasing awareness, humankind will always be evolving, always innovating, always searching for new meaning.

No doubt, we already have living examples of the Fifth Order of design. As an example, rather than defining success through an end goal, people feel success through exploration, testing, learning, creating, and challenging themselves, and actively participating as creative, thoughtful human beings. Through designing systems, people design bigger changes. Through designing awareness, the learning is holistic and the results are a mega change. This includes further evolving the critical thinking about design and design thinking to include the broader human impact—further evolving the triple bottom line and the effects of innovation on the full wellness of humanity. It is the consideration of the Fifth Order that will bring about the human-centered changes and trends of the future. Part of the current evidence is the megatrend of design thinking. More than any other of the organizational processes that

"I hope for a whole new way of problem solving (design thinking) that is here forever."

—Wendy Castleman,
Intuit

have come before it, design thinking offers the greatest opportunity to confront and innovate in response to the greatest challenges of humankind.

JUST GETTING STARTED

Throughout our research it's safe to say we've learned a lot. It's hard to conduct more than 70 interviews with experts on a topic we all share so much passion around without getting totally immersed in content and totally informed; it's been a fascinating journey. Along the way we tested many of our hypotheses; discovered many new insights; learned lots of special tips and even some secrets; found all kinds of tools, methods, processes and strategies; discovered what works and what doesn't in the mission to scale design thinking; made many great friendships; and set our point of view about building cultures of innovation.

We have truly tried to share as much as our study sample and a book of this length will permit. And we've tried to keep the content high enough to appeal to a broad range of readers. Yet, there is so much more. We'd love to go deeper with you, but this is not the time or place. This research has led to our development of many new models, tools, and techniques, such as a Design Thinking At Scale™ Framework, a Cultural Innovation Readiness™ Framework, a Design Thinking Maturity™ Model, and updates to many of our Culture Alignment tools. Practicing what we preach, this work has been co-created with users, prototyped, iterated, and is roughly ready. Though we like the idea of an MVP (minimum viable product) initially, we find it important to be in alignment with our work. Therefore, we will continue to explore innovation and creativity, and find new paths to improving what we offer here. We'll continue to empathize, define, ideate, prototype, and test.

We sincerely hope all the information in this book will empower you to take on the challenges of scaling design thinking yourselves and contribute to producing change, driving new ideas, and delivering meaningful solutions to the world.

NOTES

Chapter 1

1. We suggest two wonderful resources for better understanding the early evolution of man's ability to innovate: Yuval Noah Harari's book *Sapiens* (HarperCollins, 2015), and, if you prefer watching over reading, the documentary made-for-television series *The Great Human Odyssey*.
2. "Now or Never. Global CEO Outlook," KPMG International 2016, *https://home.kpmg.com/content/dam/kpmg/pdf/2016/06/2016-global-ceo-outlook.pdf*.
3. "Redefining Boundaries: Insights From the Global C-Suite Study," IBM, 2016, *www-01.ibm.com/common/ssi/cgi-bin/ssialias?subtype =XB&infotype=PM&htmlfid=GBE03695USEN&attachment=GBE 03695USEN.PDF*.
4. 20th Annual CEO Survey, PwC, 2016, *www.pwc.com/gx/en/ceo -agenda/ceosurvey/2017/us*.
5. "The DMI: Design Value Index," 2015, *DMI.org*.
6. John Maeda, "Design in Tech Report 2017," *www.slideshare.net/john maeda/design-in-tech-report-2017*.

Chapter 2

1. Thomas Lockwood, *Design Thinking* (New York: Allworth Press/ DMI, 2009).
2. Wikipedia, "Design Thinking," *https://en.wikipedia.org/wiki/Design _thinking*.

3. "Top 25 Most Innovative Companies 2016," *Forbes*, 2016, *www.forbes.com/pictures/elem45igi/no-22-coloplast/?ss=innovative-companies#5e868d766dbe.*

4. "Most Innovative Companies," *Fast Company*, 2017, *www.fastcompany.com/most-innovative-companies.*

5. Guadalupe Gonzalez, "The Top 10 Most Innovative Companies," *Inc.*, July 7, 2016, *www.inc.com/guadalupe-gonzalez/ss/10-smartest-companies.html.*

6. "The Most Innovative Companies of the Fortune 500," June 6, 2016, *www.surveymonkey.com/mp/measures/business/fortune-100-innovative/.*

Chapter 3

1. Edgar Papke, *True Alignment* (New York: AMACOM, 2013). For further insight into the traits and characteristics of culture, we recommend reading Chapter 8 of *True Alignment*.

2. W.C. Schutz, *FIRO: A Three-Dimensional Theory of Interpersonal Behavior* (New York: Holt, Rinehart, & Winston, 1958).

3. A.L. Hammer and E.R. Schnell, *FIRO-B® Technical Guide* (Mountain View, Calif.: CPP, Inc., 2000).

4. Wilbert Baan, "Richard Buchanan Being Interviewed About His 4 Orders of Design, Design, People and Technology, 2013, *www.wilbertbaan.nl/2013/05/17/richard-buchanan-being-interviewed-about-his-4-orders-of-design/.*

Chapter 4

1. John G. Rice, "How GE Is Becoming a Truly Global Network," *McKinsey Quarterly*, April 2017.

2. Thomas Lockwood, "Five Trends in Design Leadership," *Fast Company*, 2016, *www.fastcodesign.com/3058483/5-trends-in-design-leadership.*

3. Andrew Small, the Atlantic City Lab, retrieved from an interview with Jeff Immelt, 2016, *www.citylab.com/work/2016/09/why-ge-moved-from-bridgeport-to-boston-atlantic-ideas-forum/502061/.*

4. Steve Lohr, "GE Is Moving to Boston and Itself Into the Digital Era," *The New York Times*, January 14, 2016, *www.nytimes.com/2016/01/14/technology/ge-boston-headquarters.html?_r=0.*

5. Edgar Papke, *True Alignment* (New York: AMACOM, 2013).

Chapter 5

1. Andrew Small, the Atlantic City Lab, retrieved from an interview with Jeff Immelt, 2016, *www.citylab.com/work/2016/09/why-ge-moved-from-bridgeport-to-boston-atlantic-ideas-forum/502061/*.
2. Edgar Papke, *True Alignment* (New York: AMACOM, 2013).

Chapter 6

1. PwC, Global Innovations Study, 2017, retrieved from *www.strategy and.pwc.com/innovation1000*.
2. Roger Martin, "The Innovation Catalysts," *Harvard Business Review*, June 2011.
3. Suzanne Pellican, "Design Thinking in the Corporate DNA." Intuit, 2016.
4. Brad Smith, "Intuit's CEO on Building a Design-Driven Company," *Harvard Business Review*, January–February 2015.
5. Interview with Suzanne Pelican, 2016 O'Reilly Design Conference, retrieved from *www.youtube.com/watch?v=bJWjRad-4Mw*.
6. "Facts & Information," SAP website, 2017, retrieved from *www.sap.com/corporate/en/company.html*.

Chapter 7

1. *Marriott International Annual Report*, Morningstar Financial Reporting, 2015, *http://financials.morningstar.com/ratios/r.html?t=MAR*.
2. "Forbes' 14th Annual Global 2000: The World's Biggest Public Companies," *Forbes*, 2016.
3. "The World's Largest Public Companies 2017," *Forbes*, 2017, retrieved from *www.forbes.com/sites/corinnejurney/2017/05/24/the-worlds-largest-public-companies-2017/#380b8bb4508d*.

Chapter 8

1. "Driven by Innovation," SAP, 2017, retrieved from *www.sap.com/corporate/en/company/innovation.html*.
2. H.W.J. Rittel and M.M. Webber, *Dilemmas in a General Theory of Planning*, Policy Sciences, 1973.
3. Lin, et al., "Service Design and Change of Systems: Human-Centered Approaches to Implementing and Spreading Service Design," *International Journal of Design*, 2011.

4. "Standardized Shift-Change Process Optimizes Time for Transfer of Patient Care Responsibility, Leads to High Levels of Nurse and Patient Satisfaction," AHRQ, 2014.

Chapter 9

1. For further information regarding GE Healthcare's innovations in MR environments, we suggest reading "Design of the Times: Factoring in Patient Emotions for Future Innovations." The article reports on the Compassion Project, which focused on Caring MR Suites, a reflection of the organization's "caring hands" design philosophy, which serve to look after the emotional well-being of a patient using lighting, interior décor, scenery, and music.

Chapter 10

1. James Morehead, Stanford University's Carol Dweck on the Growth of Mindset and Education, OneDublin.org, 2012, retrieved from *https://onedublin.org/2012/06/19/stanford-universitys-carol-dweck-on-the-growth-mindset-and-education/*.
2. Tomas Chamorro-Premuzic, " Curiosity Is as Important as Intelligence," *Harvard Business Review*, 2014, retrieved from *https://hbr.org/2014/08/curiosity-is-as-important-as-intelligence*.

Chapter 11

1. Philips Annual Report 2016, retrieved from *www.philips.com/static/annualresults/2016/PhilipsFullAnnualReport2016_English.pdf*.
2. T. Amabile, C. Fisher, and J. Pellemer, "IDEO's Culture of Helping," *Harvard Business Review*, 2014, retrieved from *https://hbr.org/2014/01/ideos-culture-of-helping*.

Chapter 12

1. "At LEGO, Growth and Culture Are Not Kid Stuff: An Interview With Jørgen Vig Knudstrop," BCG, 2017, retrieved from *www.lego.com/en-us/aboutus/news-room/2016/july/new-office-building*.
2. Katherine Bisgaard Vase, "The Lego Group Shares Plans for New Office Building in Billund," 2016, retrieved from *www.lego.com/en-us/aboutus/news-room/2016/july/new-office-building*.
3. "Innovate For Children," LEGO website, 2014, retrieved from *www.lego.com/en-us/aboutus/responsibility/innovate-for-children*.

Chapter 13

1. We recommend viewing Doug Dietz's TEDx talk in which he shares the details of his story about transforming healthcare for children and their families at *www.youtube.com/watch?v=jajduxPD6H4&feature =youtu.be.*

Chapter 14

1. IBM 100, "Good Design Is Good Business; Icons of Design," IBM 100, 2017, retrieved from *www-03.ibm.com/ibm/history/ibm100/us /en/icons/gooddesign/.*
2. IBM Design, 2017, retrieved from *www.ibm.com/design/.*
3. 3M Design, 2017, retrieved from *www.3m.com/3M/en_US/design-us/.* "Q&A Eric Quint," *DMI Review, Vol. 28, No. 3,* 2017.
4. Edgar Papke, *True Alignment* (New York: AMACOM, 2013).

Chapter 15

1. J. Collins, and J. Porras, *Built to Last* (New York: HarperBusiness, 1994).
2. J&J Credo, 2017, *www.jnj.com/about-jnj/jnj-credo.*
3. Eden Ames, "Millennial Demand for Corporate Social Responsibility Drives Change in Brand Strategies," American Marketing Association, 2017, retrieved from *www.ama.org/publications/MarketingNews /Pages/millennial-demand-for-social-responsibility-changes-brand -strategies.aspx.*

INDEX